Cray Cray

*The Girl Who Climbed Out of the Cuckoo's Nest
and Found Her Way to a Thriving Heart*

Kristine Medea

© Kristine Medea.

All rights reserved. In accordance with the U.S. Copyright Act of 1976, the scanning, uploading, and electronic sharing of any part of this book without the permission of the publisher is unlawful piracy of this book and theft of intellectual property. If you would like to use material from the book (other than for review purposes), prior written permission must be obtained by contacting the publisher at Thrive@ThrivingHeart.com. Thank you for your support of the author's rights.

ThrivingHeart Healing Arts
158 Moreland Avenue, SE
Atlanta, GA 30316
Thrive@ThrivingHeart.com

Cover design by: Andrej Semnic/s e m 'n i t z
Page design & typography by: GoMyStory.com/John W Prince

Printed in the United States of America

Library of Congress Control Number: 2018944775

Medea, Kristine

Cray Cray: The Girl Who Climbed Out of the Cuckoo's Nest and Found Her Way to a Thriving Heart / Kristine Medea

The autobiography of a girl who was incarcerated in a state mental hospital at age 12, and her adult self-reconciling of that experience through her professional lens as a trauma therapist.

ISBN-13: 978-1718653290

ISBN-10: 1718653298

To sweet man
For always knowing the way home
For you

Acknowledgments

This book wouldn't have been possible without a long ride down Interstate 5 in the back seat of a VW Vanagon. Such deep gratitude to my girls Liz and Annie for taking that journey with me.

I wouldn't have been able to find the words to tell my story without the love and encouragement of my best sister friend, Liz Wall. She has patiently walked by my side through the years, as I've brought my life, and this book, to life. Thank you, Liz, for believing.

I want to give thanks to my family of choice for supporting and believing in me, and for seeing the value of sharing my story. Especially Annie Neal and Leonice Holthaus for their steadfast support, frequent research forays to the local library, and for providing me a safe place to land again and again.

A special word of gratitude to my Mom, Bev Conaway, for being brave and leading my rescue out of the storm. She showed this wild child what it is to be part of a family and knew that one more institution and I would be lost forever. Rest in peace. Thanks to my Dad, Gary Conaway, for his steady and kind heart.

With deep gratitude to Diana Arling for holding space for my healing and for welcoming me to the world. Her compassion, love, and encouragement forever changed the course of my life.

And finally, I want to give warm thanks to the ThrivingHeart team, especially Courtney King, for assembling a rock star team to support this project and the work we do to bring healing and light to our community.

– Kristine

Author's Note

All of the events and experiences chronicled in this book are true and accurate, to the best of my recollection. I apologize for any inadvertent errors in recounting any of the specific details and timelines of this story.

Some of the names of people mentioned in the book have been changed, and some of their identifying circumstances altered, to preserve confidentiality and privacy.

Contents

Introduction	1
Chapter 1: You Inherit the Pain	7
Chapter 2: If You Live Like an Animal	17
Chapter 3: The Problem Child	35
Chapter 4: Disorder in the Court	45
Chapter 5: A Star Still Shines	63
Chapter 6: The Real Cuckoo's Nest	81
Chapter 7: No Way Home	99
Chapter 8: He Was Going to Teach Me What Real Love Is	111
Chapter 9: In the Womb, Part I	127
Chapter 10: A Kid in Grown-up's Clothing	139
Chapter 11: Hand on the Telephone	153
Chapter 12: In the Womb, Part II	165
Chapter 13: Graduation Day	179
Chapter 14: The Cowgirl Rides Again	191
Chapter 15: No Bad Apples	201
Afterword	209

Cray Cray

Introduction

It happens to most of us. Some time in our adult lives, we feel an urgent need to go back and revisit those places in our childhood that we once called home. We yearn to find out if that old familiar environment is still the way we remembered it, or if it has changed almost beyond recognition. In our eagerness to recapture vital memories, we touch the walls, gaze up at the ceilings, peer out the windows, and open every closed door. We've got to have images to take back, reminders of what was. We hunger to make meaning of it all. Our homes shaped our identity, helped to make us who we are. No matter what we've done or where we've gone since we left, we can't help but tap into that pull to reconnect and remember.

That's especially true if your home for a vulnerable period of childhood happens to have been a state mental hospital.

So, when I was 40 years old and heard that the home that probably had the most influence on my life was about to be torn down, I had to take action. I dashed off an email to Oregon State Senator Peter Courtney:

My name is Kristine Medea and I currently reside in Atlanta, Georgia. However, I was born and raised in Oregon. In 1976, after some time in mental health care, I was admitted to Ward 40A of the Oregon State Hospital Child & Adolescent

Kristine Medea

Secure Treatment Unit. I was 12 years old.

Needless to say, the experience has had long-lasting effects on me, including my decision for my career. I currently am a psychotherapist and child advocate. I am passionate about my work, specializing in the area of trauma recovery and resolution. I have worked long and hard to make sense of the trauma I experienced as a child resulting from institutionalized care.

I have tried for a number of years to gain access to the building in an attempt to affirm my childhood experiences and memories there, but to no avail. There is no class reunion for the children of Oregon State Hospital, no way to connect with others to remember and make meaning of that time in my life. The cloak of confidentiality leaves me alone to make sense of it all.

It is my understanding that the Child & Adolescent Treatment program has been closed and that McKenzie Hall, the building I lived in, is slated to be torn down. That is why I am asking for your help to gain access to Ward 40A before it is gone. I just want the opportunity to see this place where I lived, one more time before it is too late.

I directed my plea to State Senator Courtney because he had been instrumental in the move to shut down operations at Oregon State Hospital in response to newspaper articles exposing a long history of sexual abuse inflicted on adolescent patients, as well as the decrepit conditions of the historic old building. If anyone could pull strings to get me inside Ward 40A, I figured he could. But would he?

His email response was immediate, a rarity for elected officials. "I will do everything I can to get you back inside the Oregon State Hospital" was the gist of his message, and the next morning I got a phone call from an administrative staff member of Oregon State Hospital. I was going home!

Within days, I was on a plane from Atlanta to Seattle, and then on a midnight drive down to Portland. With two of my dearest friends for support, and a VW van with a portable fridge stocked with my favorite drinks in the back, I headed for Salem at the break of day. We pulled into the sprawling grounds, reined in by the mammoth fences turned inward at the top to prevent escape. People all across the U.S. would

Cray Cray

recognize those grounds from vivid scenes in the popular 1970s Jack Nicholson movie *One Flew Over the Cuckoo's Nest*, which happened to have been filmed at Oregon State Hospital just a year prior to my arrival there. But there was nothing fictitious about this mental hospital to me. This Cuckoo's Nest is a real place; I've got the scars to prove it.

I took a deep breath. As I climbed the steps toward the entrance, I noticed the same buzzer box that my Children Services caseworker Cecily pushed that day when I was a scared and lonely but feisty 12-year-old girl that had been sent off to a state hospital because she was too "emotionally disturbed" to live with her family. She was the "sick" one, the crazy kid, truly "cray cray." And now the door was about to be opened that would usher me back into that time and place, my world, my home…

This book will zoom the camera in on what I unearthed during my revisit inside Ward 40A of Oregon State Hospital that day, and it will take you further back and follow the trail along all the days, months and years when I wrestled with the label of a mental patient. I'm going to provide a close-up look at the trauma and horrors I experienced growing up as an outcast child, a fighter, a throwaway. I will show you all the ways I was poked, prodded and pathologized, and how that treatment left its mark on me. I will escort you into places and experiences I have tried hard to forget and reveal moments when the struggle to enter adulthood alive and intact showed no promise for anything other than a tragic ending.

But I made it out of that experience alive and intact, and I found my way to a thriving heart. Sometimes I still wonder how. I've built a life in which I am surrounded by people I love, those who know and embrace me for who I am and what I have lived through. I'm emotionally and psychologically healthy, and spiritually fulfilled. As a psychotherapist and founder of ThrivingHeart Healing Arts Associates in Atlanta, I cherish the opportunity to stand beside and assist others who are suffering the effects of trauma or who have begun the steep climb toward hope and healing. I try to apply what I have learned, not only as one who personally experienced acute trauma but as someone who has witnessed first-hand what is and is not helpful and effective in the professional treatment of children, adolescents and adults in pain. I am proud to call myself a child advocate, welcoming forums to promote needed changes in our mental health system.

In some ways, I'm still sorting out the full impact of being raised in the mental health system. Writing this book has turned over new clues and sparked fresh revelations, and even raised more questions. I don't have all the answers; still, I invite you to accompany me on this journey of reflection, where I will share what I have lived and learned. If you are knee-deep in your own trauma, or seeking to summon the strength to begin your journey, my hope is that you may find within my words some kernel of truth, a voice of understanding and support, a glimmer of hope or encouragement. Even if you are not yet able to see your path to health and healing, I will hold the space of possibility for you.

Others who have turned to this book may already have forged their way to a healthier and more fulfilling place. If you have somehow survived and even thrived after something bad happened to you, then you may gain a deeper awareness and appreciation for how far you've come and who and what contributed to your growth.

If you are the loved one of someone in pain, I applaud your commitment to seek guidance and hope, whether that person you care about happens to be a child, an adolescent or an adult. I also welcome those in the healthcare professions, especially people with a hands-on role in working with our vulnerable younger population. I trust that you will join with me in advocating for a more aware, compassionate and loving approach in aiding those young people who may be suffering not only their own personal pain but the added trauma that so often comes with being labeled or stigmatized.

It may sound strange to say so, but I am grateful for everything that I have lived through. One way or another, all my experiences, even the most traumatic ones, have helped to shape me. They have made me who I am and enabled me to find my place, and my voice, in trying to make a positive contribution to the world around us. Even in my darkest hours, I always had a fighting spirit, and now that spirit has evolved into a strength—a strength that gives me the courage to come face to face with the hopelessness and helplessness of places and people I once called home.

1
You Inherit the Pain

If you live around Portland, Oregon, you get used to day after day of gray skies, intermittent rain and a chill that drives you to wrap yourself in sweaters and scarfs. The weather seeps into your bones, becomes part of you. For my entire childhood and early adulthood, that gray, dark, dismal, sputtering-rain weather was a reflection of how I often felt inside.

I can't say for sure, since I was only four years old at the time, but I bet it was on one of those gray, dreary days when I approached the open bathroom door and saw my mother standing in front of the toilet. We had a tiny bathroom, just room enough for a sink, toilet and bathtub, and when the door opened to the inside most of the remaining space was eaten up. When I was close enough to see her scrunched in there, she glanced at me before sobbing words that have remained seared in my brain ever since.

"I'm sorry. I'm sorry. I'm sorry."

I was confused. What was my mother doing? And then I saw her take out the knife. As my hand reached up to cover my mouth, terrified, I watched her begin to slash up and down on both her arms. Whoosh, whoosh, whoosh. Almost silent. Within seconds, blood was spilling onto the floor of that tiny bathroom and seeping toward the hallway where I was standing. I began screaming and I didn't let up while I ran out of the house, crossed the street and raced into the neighbor lady's house.

"My mommy, my mommy, my mommy!" I yelled, my arms outstretched.

The neighbor lady paused just long enough to lay her hand on my head. "Stay here!" she ordered. "Just stay put."

After she scurried toward our house to investigate what had terrified me, my sobbing eased. A couple of minutes later, I saw the flashing red lights of the police cruiser outside our house, with the ambulance following close behind. My mother's gruesome attempt to end her life had failed, and after being treated for her injuries, she was locked away in Dammasch State Hospital in Wilsonville.

My younger sister and I were sent to live with my grandparents, and not for the first time. My mother was an alcoholic, following in my grandmother's footsteps, and she also suffered from anorexia and bulimia. When she wasn't starving herself, she would be binging and purging. On the day she gave birth to me in 1964, she weighed all of 86 pounds, as the story goes. So, on those occasions when her psychological state reached the out-of-control point, I would be shipped to her parents' house for some extended period while she went off somewhere for some kind of treatment. This time she was going to be gone much longer than usual.

My father had already bailed out of our home life, ending a marriage that by all accounts was a disaster. My parents met while they were students at Franklin High School in southeast Portland. My dad was an All-American athlete in football, basketball and wrestling, where he was a teammate of my mother's brother. They got engaged right out of high school, and I was conceived soon after the wedding. Their troubles arose early on. As my uncle confided in me later, my mother "had a hard time being married," a polite way of saying she was sleeping around. I guess that along with alcoholism and bulimia she also must have been struggling with the idea of being a mother, because somehow or other I wound up being left unattended for long periods of time while she was out drinking, or doing whatever. Once I was left alone in my crib for many hours, days I was told, before the lady across the street heard my crying and screaming and found me covered in a terrible rash. That was another episode that ended with me being carted off to my grandparents' house.

My parents did stay together long enough to bring my younger sister Karen into the world, which meant that there were now two children being neglected. In one of my earliest childhood memories, I am listening to my baby sister screeching with hunger. Realizing that I am the only one around to feed her, I drag a chair over to the kitchen countertop, then stretch and strain to reach the cupboard so I can pull down the big yellow box of Cheerios.

We lived in a one-story red house with a cyclone fence around it and a front yard with no trees. You could call our house messy. Hell, it was rat-infested. I had been warned never to open the door to the laundry room because rats were sometimes known to prowl there, but one night I awoke and found my parents gone. Alone on the sofa, I was cold, so I opened the laundry room door to retrieve some clean and dry clothes to cover myself, winding up with a rat bite on the inside of my thigh and a morbid fear of rats that I have never outgrown.

My parents' marital troubles came to a head one night in a scene played out near the front door of our house. Lying on the hardwood floor of my bedroom, I could just make out what was happening. They were yelling, as usual, and my mother was intoxicated, as usual. What was different this time was that my father was smashing my mother's head with his fist. Apparently, he had caught her in bed with her latest lover. I thought he was going to kill her, but as it turned out the only thing that died that night was the marriage.

So, there I was back at my grandparents' home, carrying the fresh, vivid image of my mother slashing herself with a knife. On another one of those cloudy days, I was sitting by the kitchen counter when I noticed the bottle of baby aspirin my grandmother kept for us. I reached into the bottle, scooped out a few of the chewable tablets and quickly devoured them. "Yum, tastes like candy," I said to myself, savoring the orangey taste. "I think I'll have some more." By the time my grandmother walked in, the bottle was almost empty.

She didn't yell, she just looked at the bottle and then at me. The expression on her face told me that I was in trouble. I assumed that my offense was sneaking around and chowing down all that orange "candy," but the way my grandmother frantically surged into action made it clear that I was wrong. This time the flashing red lights were coming for me!

Next thing I knew, I was lying in the emergency room with tubes running down my body. Even though they had to pump my stomach, I do not believe that I was intentionally trying to mimic my mother's suicidal behavior. Then again, parental modeling does go in pretty deep.

Despite this baby aspirin incident, my grandparents decided that I was an excellent candidate for preschool. I disagreed, not only because I derived at least some comfort from being in their presence but also because on the morning they picked to send me off to school for the first time, I was deeply engrossed in watching *Romper Room*.

"Okay, Kristy, time to go to school," my grandmother said sweetly. "Time to get your coat on."

"No, I don't want to go!" I shouted, and I refused to budge from my TV-viewing perch.

"Come on now, Kristy. You have to go," she replied, this time not so sweetly.

I got up, raced into the dining room and wrapped my arms and legs around one of the legs of the dining table. My grandmother and grandfather joined forces, yanking at my limbs to pry me loose. They had made their decision about what to do with me, and they were not backing down. Neither was I.

"I don't want to go! No, I don't want to go!" I shouted, and because I was a strong little girl, as many other adults would soon discover, it took them a while to separate me from the dining table leg. Eventually, my grandparents won the tug-of-war and I found myself in a preschool classroom sitting on one of those wooden toddler chairs with the woven seats. Right from the start, my favorite activity while seated on my chair was to push myself backwards until my head banged against the floor. As soon as my head got smacked, I would quickly set the chair back up neatly in its place and then proceed to push myself back and slam my head on the floor again. While the preschool staff members were left to wonder what on earth I was trying to do, I found my little routine quite soothing. There was something about the rhythm of the backward movement and the banging of my head that answered some need. I would not have been able to explain it then, but I guess I was seeking a sense of rhythm and routine in a life full of chaos and unpredictability. And things were just getting started.

After my grandparents realized that their troubled daughter would not be coming out of the state hospital to reclaim their two granddaughters for several months, they made it clear that they were not signing on to an indefinite parenting plan. That's when they turned to their son-in-law.

"You're the dad. You have a responsibility here," they argued. "You need to come and get your girls now."

My dad agreed, although I was later told that he wasn't driven solely by a strong sense of parental duty. This was the late 1960s, with the Vietnam War intensifying, and from what I understand, my dad's status as a full-time active parent for children whose mother was not available had a positive impact on his draft status. All I knew was that I did not like this plan one bit. I wanted to stay with my grandparents, not so I could repeat the tug-of-war at the dining table every morning but because I wanted to be with my mom. Her mother and father seemed like the closest thing to having her, so that's what I wanted to hold onto. But I didn't get a vote.

At first, my sister and I lived with my dad in his elderly grandmother's home. His family, like my mom's, was deeply rooted in Oregon, with traces of Portland malaise in his heritage, too. My great-grandfather was once the master gardener for the Portland Rose Garden, one of the city's main attractions since the 1920s. While tending to those

10,000 roses, he was known to take a nip, or more than a nip. Many a morning he would be found passed out among the roses, or in some less beatific parts of the city. My grandmother, the rose gardener's daughter, suffered from narcolepsy, which she treated with amphetamines to keep her awake, and benzodiazepines to bring her down. One of my father's brothers survived his service in Vietnam only to come home bearing the physical effects of Agent Orange, and a heroin addiction.

My great-grandmother liked to cook popcorn over an open fire, allowing the popcorn to pop freely all over the living room. I thought that was the funniest thing I had ever seen. She also happened to be diabetic, so I had to get used to the taste of sugar-free hot chocolate. At least she was nice enough to keep a small bowl of butterscotch candy for my sister and me. I was munching on those butterscotch candies on the day that my father told me my mother was coming to visit. While I waited and watched for hours, snow began to fall outside.

"Well, the roads are probably getting really bad," my father said. "She might not be able to make it."

That just made me start to cry, although I managed to keep eating the candy. I was keeping a constant vigil looking out the window, and suddenly a vision appeared: a figure approaching the house on the back of a horse.

"It's her! Mommy, mommy!" I yelled and rushed toward the front door, not stopping to figure out how my mother could be riding a horse on the city streets of Portland. Yet this was no child's fantasy. My mother did love horses and she had really come, riding on her horse Salam in the snow. After she unbundled herself from her hat, coat and gloves, she presented me with a coloring book and a box of crayons. For 30 magical minutes, I sat by the hearth of the fireplace coloring and talking to my mother. Then, as if signaled by a jail warden that the family visit time had expired, she got up to leave. "Got to get the horse back to the barn," she explained, and I watched her image on that horse's back fade in the distant snow.

"She'll come see you again soon," my father assured me, but he wasn't

Cray Cray

fooling me. My mother's presence in my life to that point had never been consistent or dependable, and as much as I yearned for that to change, I had no choice but to focus on my present situation. And that wasn't very consistent either. Soon my father was moving again, this time to an old Victorian house in Portland. He rented the third floor, with the Anderson family occupying the main part of the house. As part of the arrangement, Mrs. Anderson looked after Karen and me during the day while my dad worked.

I found things to like about this house, especially the swinging doors and the laundry chute that went from the upper floors to the basement. The washer and dryer were down there, and so was Mr. Anderson's workshop. He was a woodworker, always busy with some creative project.

My dad at least spent some time with us at night. I remember his routine of chasing the two of us around while doing his Jimmy Cagney impression: "You dirty rats! I'm going to get you!" Karen and I would scream and pretend to try to get away, while staying close enough for him to catch us. When he did, he would immediately start tickling us, which made us squeal. It's one of the best memories I have of my dad.

I enjoyed those moments when my father's playful spirit shone through, but most of the time he took a strict approach. Obedience was always expected. He would spank me sometimes, although at least I knew what I had done to cross his boundary lines. As a former high school jock, he only seemed comfortable around us during some kind of shared physical activity. "Let's go ice skating!" he would say, and he'd whisk us off to the skating rink in the atrium of the Lloyd Center, Portland's large indoor mall where Olympian Tonya Harding first learned to skate. Or he'd say, "Let's go play kickball" and lead us outside. He bought me my first bicycle and showed me how to ride it. He was probably doing his best at parenting, but he was ill-equipped to provide the kind of emotional bonding and compassionate understanding that I needed. That's why I still wanted my mother and, somehow, I still believed she was going to show up and deliver what I craved—not for half an hour here and there but for each and every waking day of my life.

In the meantime, I was beginning to find ways to test my dad's limits. I especially didn't like change, so the adjustment to starting kindergarten as a five-year-old was scary for me. I didn't like the hours I spent in the care of Mrs. Anderson, either, although she was a nice enough lady. And the day my dad left me with a teenage babysitter, a girl I didn't even know, my blood was boiling. I'm sure that this young girl had her hands full with me that day, though I don't remember specifically what set me off. I do remember what happened after my dad came home and he and the babysitter sat down to talk on the front porch—without me. I wanted to be with my dad.

"No, Kristy," he said as I stormed out to the porch, bursting past the screen door with a glass section in it. "Go wait in the house until I'm finished."

Wait? No way! In response to my father's command, I punched out the glass part of the door. All the way home from the emergency room, where I received too many stitches for me to count, he seethed in silence. I'd never seen him so mad. I was scared of what would happen next.

I retreated to my room. Stroking my bandaged hand and arm, I felt deflated and defeated. I want my mom, I thought to myself, *I have to find my mom*. But I didn't even know where she was. Was she still in the hospital? Did she have a new home somewhere far away?

Then I figured that if I could not have my mom right away, at least I could get away from my dad and all his rules and yelling, and kindergarten, and people I didn't want to be around. *I'll run away, that's what I'll do*, I thought. I was smart—I knew that I needed a plan. I considered the options for a nice place to live and remembered those moments when we'd go ice skating at the Lloyd Center. I would like it there, I decided. No one would know me in the mall. "That's it, I'll go live at the Lloyd Center!" I said to myself, and without bothering to take anything at all, I boldly descended the two flights of stairs from our third-floor dwelling and walked right out the front door. I had pulled off my escape without my dad even noticing.

I walked and walked for what must have been 20 blocks, somehow figuring out the way. I arrived at the Lloyd Center and calmly claimed a bench to watch the ice skaters. I relaxed into my new home, in no hurry to decide what to do or where to go next, just enjoying the peace from having no one to tell me what to do.

The peace ended when two adults came over and sat down beside me.

"Where's your mother, little girl?" one of them asked, gazing down at my arm wrapped in gauze.

"I don't know," I answered honestly. "If I knew where she was, that's where I would be right now instead of sitting here talking to you."

"I see," the other man said softly. "Well then, where is your father?"

"I'm not sure, but he's probably still at the house…it's not really our house, we just share it," I explained.

"Do you know his telephone number?" the first one asked, and I said I didn't, which was true. By then I had figured out that these people had something to do with the Lloyd Center and that their arrival was not good news for me. Somehow, they must have tracked down my dad because it wasn't long before he showed up at the skating rink. And I could tell from his expression that he was not amused. It was clear we were not going skating today.

"Kristy, how could you do this?" he began as soon as he got me alone in the car. "What were you even thinking? Didn't you know that some bad man could have come and just taken you away? Kristy, what am I going to do with you?"

Well, I knew my dad didn't have an answer to his own question. I also knew that he was completely incapable of understanding *why* I had run away and what I really needed. He had no idea how to calm me when I got upset, no grasp for what was causing my anxiety.

I did my best to get on with my life in this home that wasn't really our home, with a family that wasn't really our family, and a kindergarten with rules that I didn't want to follow because all I really wanted was to be somewhere else.

"Your mom got remarried," my dad announced one day. It had been about a year and a half since she had turned that knife on herself and got whisked off to the state hospital. I had seen her only once since that day she showed up at our door riding a horse in the snow, and that was with another boyfriend. This guy was apparently someone new.

"Yes, she's married to a nice man, a really nice man," my father added. "And they're coming here soon to take you out for a visit."

Wow, Mom's coming. And she's with a nice man! Maybe we can be together for more than a few minutes this time. I was flushed with hope.

2
If You Live Like an Animal

The "nice man" made a good first impression. He and my mother, looking beautiful in a new dress, pulled up in a big, shiny white Buick, with a light blue interior and a huge steering wheel. After we had driven out of Portland and into the country, my mother's new husband, Jack, steered us into an A&W Root Beer drive-in. I thought it was amazing that they brought your hamburgers right to your car window on a tray, and my sister and I loved our kid-sized A&W root beer mugs. After we ate, Jack sat me right at the steering wheel. I looked at his striped, hip-hugger pants, quite stylish at the time. *Wow, he's very cool*, I thought.

We continued on our way, out into the suburbs to the town of Hillsboro, before turning onto his family's property. As I would soon learn, Jack's father used to run a lumber manufacturing plant there before he died. Most of the buildings of the shut-down business remained, and his mother still lived there. Apparently, my mother and Jack were living there with her. As they showed us around, my mind drifted to all the ways Karen and I could find to play around these old abandoned buildings. At one point on our orientation tour, Jack ran ahead and jumped out from inside one of the buildings wearing a bear skin. I got a little scared by that, but it seemed like a sign that he liked to have fun.

They guided us into their beautiful, two-bedroom, knotty-pine house and brought us to the upstairs attic area that felt like a fort. I noticed stacks and stacks of *National Geographic* magazines along one side of the space.

"Do you like it?" my mother asked. "This is your new home."

New home? Wait, this is just a visit!

And then I understood. My dad had lied to me about just going off on a visit, and my mother and this man she married purposely didn't tell us that we would be living here until we had already arrived. And this man I had just met was going to be *living* with me as my *stepfather!*

"What? What do you mean?" I said. Confused, I wanted to be with my mom, but not this man. But I had no say in the matter, just as I had no input into being shipped off to my grandparents' home every time my mom wound up in a mental hospital, or being shuttled around Portland by my father. I would just have to deal with the situation…for now.

I did kind of like Jack's mother, whom we were told to call "Mumsy." She was a very proper looking woman who used to be an executive secretary with the lumber business. I thought her IBM electric typewriter was the coolest thing. After I would beg her to let me use it, she would sometimes allow me to sit at the keyboard and bang out my gibberish.

Upstairs in our private fort, I loved looking through the *National Geographics,* carefully studying the pictures of how people from all over the world lived. I started dreaming of what it would be like to live somewhere far, far away, and soon created my own way of finding out. I would tear out some of those pictures and take them with me out on the property. When I came to a rusted out pickup truck, I would sit at the wheel and imagine that I was driving off to one of those exotic locations.

Russia was my favorite landing place. Day after day, I would sit at the wheel of that pickup, the best toy a kid could have, with an old towel wrapped around the top of my head pretending I was a Russian Babushka. For a change of pace, I would imagine that I was driving through the South. I would become the classic Southern woman, talking to Karen in my best Southern accent as we sipped our imaginary iced tea and ate our delicately cut sandwiches out on the veranda of some old Southern mansion.

It was natural child's fantasy play, but after a short time in this new home my get-away rides on that rusted out pickup began to serve as a necessary escape from reality. My mother may have had a different husband but she wasn't much different as a mother. My sister and I were still neglected most of the time. And this "nice man" was soon revealing himself to be, well, mean. Very mean.

While my father had been a teetotaler, Jack was my mother's drinking buddy. His behavior was on display regularly, even when we would go off on family camping trips. The newly married couple never seemed to like the idea of having two little girls tagging along, so part of their camping plan was to find ways to shove us off to the side. My mother and Jack didn't go camping to camp, they went camping to drink. They would take Karen and I to the public campgrounds up at Gales Creek, out toward the Oregon coast, or to other pretty nature spots and, after parking the car close to our site, they would set up two tents: one for them and one for us two kids. Even before dark, they would swoosh us away and get down to serious drinking.

As the night wore on, their talking would get louder and louder. That's when the fighting would kick in. When Jack got drunk, he got furious. I didn't ever see him hit my mother, but I was terrified from the start that someday he would hurt her, and hurt me too. Sometimes the police showed up at our campsite, because someone complained about the drunken commotion.

At home, whether drunk or sober, my stepfather found many more opportunities to demonstrate his not-so-nice character. Years later I would learn that Jack had suffered a severe head injury back in college in a car accident he barely survived. I don't know if that explained his behavior, but as a kid I wasn't spending any time looking for explanations. I was too busy protecting and defending myself.

Almost from the day I arrived, my stepfather would tease and taunt me mercilessly. He would make fun of me for my weight, my smell, and especially my pattern of wetting the bed. He called me every name he could imagine. "Oscar the Grouch" from *Sesame Street* was one of his favorites because he told me I looked and acted like somebody who lived in a garbage can. He'd spend so much time calling me things like "Fatty" or "Pee House" that anyone visiting our home would never know my real name was Kristy. I wasn't actually sharing the house with a stepfather. I was living with a tormentor.

Of course, I did not submit to his taunting silently. "Stop it!" I'd shout. Or "Leave me alone! I hate you!" Jack would just keep taunting me, repeating over and over how fat I was, when I was only a few pounds overweight for a girl of six or seven. Or he'd scrunch up his face and say, "You're disgusting!" He loved trying to provoke me—he thought it was funny—and I usually didn't disappoint him. I would wind up yelling and screaming at him in outbursts that would go on and on until I retreated to my upstairs fort to escape. One time I was so angry with Jack that when I got upstairs, I took a nail and gouged away chunks of the wall.

My mom's response to this verbal abuse and mistreatment her daughter was suffering at the hands of her new husband was to ignore it. She often wasn't there to witness his behavior anyway since she worked the early shift at the Pizza Caboose and he worked nights at a dog food manufacturing plant. But even when she did witness or hear about what was going on, she seemed completely indifferent to what it was doing to my emotional well-being and my sense of identity.

On one typical night of enduring Jack's taunting, I had retreated to my bed in the fort and began scribbling words of protest in my little notebook: "I hate him hate him hate him. I want her to divorce him...." In a rare gesture of support, my mom came to my room to check on me. I took this opportunity to plead my case.

"Why did you ever marry him?" I asked. "Why can't it just be us? Why can't you divorce him right *now*?"

Her response was to pick up the notebook in which I had been spouting my rage and look closely at my words.

"Oh, Kristy," she said, "you have such beautiful handwriting."

That's it. No gentle stroking of my hair, no warm hugs, no words of comfort and certainly no vow to do everything in her power to protect her daughter and stop the flood of abuse. No, all I got was a stronger reinforcement that I would have to keep going out back to the rusty old pickup truck and drive off to some far-away place where the people stood up for me and wanted me around. I was an unwanted, wild, rageful child, left to raise myself.

At least my dad had not abandoned me completely. After sending Karen and I off for that "visit" with my mom and stepfather, he would come by every other Sunday to take us for a ride in his black Chevy station wagon. Rather than taunt or tease me, my dad would express concern about my weight and disheveled appearance. My sister and I usually managed to have fun on these Dad outings. He would put the seats down in the back and we'd sit there curled up in our little blankets and play "ship." Since it was usually raining, it didn't take much imagination to pretend we were being tossed about during a nasty storm at sea. It was and still is a rare sweet memory of my childhood.

One Sunday it was not raining when we piled into the back of my dad's Chevy station wagon. Since it was a warm and sunny summer day, the windows were rolled down to let the wind blow in. Instead of battling the waves in our ship, I was sitting up and looking out intently as we cruised along the Tualatin Valley Highway. Suddenly, I heard a police siren. It was coming from behind us and when my dad slowed the station wagon and began to pull to the side the way you're supposed to do, the police car moved in close behind us.

What's wrong? Why are the police coming after Dad, I thought. But I said nothing. As my dad stepped out of our car, a second police cruiser was pulling up. I lost sight of Dad as he was guided behind both police cruisers. Karen began to cry. "It's okay," I said, taking her hand. My sister was about four and I was seven. "Dad will be all right. We just have to wait until they finish talking to him."

Well, we waited and waited and waited some more until I looked out the rear window and noticed Dad being put in handcuffs. Maybe it wasn't going to be okay after all. And then, after watching them nudge my dad into the cop car, I saw two policemen start walking toward our car. Toward...*us!*

"You girls come with me," said the cop opening the door to the station wagon.

My dad was seated on the passenger side of the back seat of the cruiser, and Karen was escorted to the middle. I sat beside her on the driver's side. So there we were—a father and his two daughters stashed in the back of a cop car with two police officers up front. Feeling the strong urge to pee, I shut my eyes tight and concentrated. If I could just hold it in until we got to the station. When the floodgates opened, I did the only thing that I could think of that made sense to do. I kept quiet. *Maybe nobody will notice*, I thought.

I was expecting to be riding down unfamiliar roads until we got to a police station, so I was surprised when, after a few miles, things were beginning to look more and more familiar. We were headed to my mother's house. "Oh, they're going to drop me and Karen home before they take Dad to jail," I said to myself, which was not a comforting thought because I was sure that Jack would be furious about me peeing in the police car.

Well, that's not exactly the way it went down. As our police car approached my mother's house, they pulled up next to another police car that was already there. There was a man in the back of that black-and-white cruiser, too. I recognized the hat right away. It was Jack's.

"Where's my mom? Where's my mom?" I screamed as they opened the back door and let Karen and I out. Our two cops didn't answer, and instead just walked us toward the front door of our house. Before we got there, another cop came out from inside. Closing the door shut behind him, he held up his hands and said, "Hold on!"

Mom's dead! I thought. *Jack killed her!* I knew that he kept a whole bunch of guns in his gun case in the living room, and I was always scared when he was anywhere near them. Terrified, I started screaming so loud that I forgot for a moment that I had peed my pants.

Cray Cray

Looking around the outside of the house for any sign of my mother, I noticed that the windows to the living room had been smashed out. I couldn't make sense of it. Someone had blown out those living room windows, and as I glanced around further I noticed that someone had blown out the dining room windows too.

"Where's Mom?!" I begged. I watched the policeman who had come out of the house rush back in, and a moment later my mom was opening the front door and stepping outside, with that same policeman right behind her. He was carrying two rifles.

I bolted toward my mom's side, but she barely paused long enough for a half-hearted squeeze before marching Karen and I directly to a neighbor's house. No longer screaming, I managed a quick peek at the surreal scene: my dad in one cop car and my stepdad in another cop car, side by side, in front of our house. And me still in wet pants.

"Don't worry," my mother said as she prepared to head off. "I'm going to the jail, and I'll get him out."

I didn't answer but to myself I said, "What? Why are you going to get my stepfather out of jail? He just shot the house up!"

And yet, that's exactly what she did. My mother went right to the police station, and as promised she bailed out my stepdad. For good measure, she also bailed out my dad.

I never did find out what my dad had been arrested for, although I believe that his problems with the cops and Jack's blowing out the windows of our house were separate, unrelated incidents. When I was older and would think back to that day, I figured that my dad must have had an outstanding warrant for something he had done before that incident. I chalked it up to an unsolved mystery.

With Jack, I didn't know for sure what had set him off, although I did know he was drunk that day. I had seen his drunken fury directed at me, at my mother, at his family during family reunions where everyone seemed to be drunk, and even at people he barely knew when something ticked him off in public. He liked to antagonize people. To step near

Jack when he had been drinking was to walk on land mines.

It's possible that my stepfather, like my father before him, had caught my mother with some other man and had chosen this particular way to tell her to "Knock it off!" I don't know because after that day they just repaired the windows and got on with day-to-day life. The father-stepfather dual arrest and gun show was never spoken of again. Even when I got a little older and Jack decided he was going to open up the gun case and take me out to learn how to properly handle and shoot with those same rifles, there was no reference made to the day he had used the living room windows for target practice.

For better or worse, I was beginning to grow up. There may have been neglect, rage and abuse all around, but at least we usually had plenty of food in the house. Not that it had much to do with any parental commitment to provide us two kids with proper nourishment. It had more to do with my mother's eating disorder. We ate lots and lots of fried chicken, although she would include a salad to create some sense of a balanced meal. We also had a constant supply of sweets. Cakes and cookies were readily available, and the crumble cakes reserved for my stepfather's "lunch" during his night shifts really caught my eye. I managed to sneak a bunch of them up to my room and, after eating them all, I would hide the wrappers. I knew that I was risking his fury if I ever got caught.

Food offered one of the few ways for my mother and I to share time together. She wouldn't do her most serious binging at home, which meant frequent road trips. Rather than binge and purge alone, she would sometimes take me along for company. So off we'd go from one food-supply source to another. On a typical food hunt, my mother might start at some burger joint, like the local Portland legend Humdinger Drive-In. She would buy six hamburgers and four milkshakes, and she would invite me to stuff down my share while chomping through her own hefty portions. After cleaning our plates at the burger joint, she would drive us along the Tualatin Valley Highway to her favorite Chinese restaurant, where she would fill up on sweet and sour pork, fried shrimp, fried rice and other favorites. Of course, before she left she would also order a couple of take-out meals. "Dinner for my family," she would say with a grin. I didn't see her purging at the ladies' rooms of those restaurants, but at home I would often find remnants of her vomiting in the bathroom.

"Now don't tell Jack about this," she would tell me during our binge runs. Sometimes, while waiting for her to finish her business in the ladies' room, I would think back to the visit I had with her and her boyfriend before Jack. One morning she took me with her to pick him up at the railroad yard where he worked nights and then drove us to a dentist's office. I can still remember hearing my mother's screams while I sat in the waiting room, and I have a vivid image of her swollen face when she stumbled out of the dentist's chair. She had all her teeth yanked out that day, no doubt a result of her chronic purging.

When my mom and I weren't out on binge runs, we might be hanging out at the Pizza Caboose. While she let me drink all the soda I wanted and gave me money for the juke box, she would drink her beer and talk to me. Rather than turning aggressive when she drank like my stepfather did, my mom would launch into great philosophical bantering. As she would talk, and talk, and talk some more about her problems and the world's problems, I listened attentively, as if I understood everything she was talking about. I was like a little adult, her designated drinking companion.

I never adopted my mother's binging and purging behavior, not that my daily life was entirely free of compulsive eating. When I was a Girl Scout, a status I somehow achieved after failing at being a Bluebird and a Brownie, I willingly accepted my assignment to sell Girl Scout cookies. I did okay going door-to-door taking orders, but when the cookies arrived for distribution my mom decided to keep them in my closet until it was time for me to deliver them.

Big mistake. After spending hours eyeing boxes and boxes of my favorite Girl Scout mint cookies, I had to taste a few of them myself. Within a few days, the taste test was complete. All the boxes were empty. Despite my mother's history with food, she didn't show any empathy. "You're going to have to tell the Girl Scouts what you did," she said. "And you'll have to find a way to work out what you owe them, because I'm not paying for them." I don't know what I did to settle things with the Girl Scouts, but to this day I still love those Girl Scout thin mint cookies and buy them whenever I come across a display where girls are selling them.

While my mother certainly was not rising up as a nurturing parent, it was my stepfather that kept me on edge. I never knew when and where the next verbal assault would come. Even after starting school, I was still "Fatty" or "Oscar the Grouch" or "Pee House."

Then one day I did something that gave him an excuse to call me by a new name. It happened one Friday, the night every week when my mother and stepfather could coordinate their schedules and go out drinking together. At that time, he would leave his change on the living room mantel: quarters, dimes, nickels and a penny jar. I usually didn't pay much attention to all that money in plain sight, but on this particular Friday evening, when they had left me alone with Karen as they often did, I heard that distinctive music blaring the coming arrival of the candy man. Suddenly, my eyes fixated on those stacks of coins. My sister and I deserved treats for putting up with being neglected, and I had the means of obtaining them. When I grabbed the stack of quarters off the mantel, I tried to convince myself that Jack would never notice them missing. I rushed out to meet the truck and bought us snow cones, cotton candy and whatever else Jack's money could afford.

I was in bed when they got home, but I could hear them arguing in their usual shared drunken state. Seconds after their loud voices stopped, I heard his footsteps coming down the hall. *Shit, maybe he noticed those quarters missing after all.* Bursting into my room, my stepfather yanked me off the bed by my feet.

"Thief!" he screamed. "You stole my money!"

"No, I didn't...what money?" I stammered.

"Liar!" he shot back. I gasped when he pulled off his belt. Thwack! "Thief!" he screamed again as he lashed out at my body a second time, and then a third time. "Liar!" he yelled again, and then he added on a few more names that I could no longer decipher. He just kept beating me and beating me with that brown belt, and when he was finished with me, my back and arms were black and blue and covered with welts.

The remnants of my stepfather's handiwork were still visible on Monday morning when I went off to join my third-grade class at Witch Hazel Elementary School. A teacher must have noticed because I was sent to the school nurse.

"Kristy, what happened to you?" she asked. "Did someone hurt you?"

"Oh, no, I just fell while I was playing outside," I answered.

The nurse or principal called my mother and stepfather in. When they arrived, and my bruises and welts were pointed out to them, they were asked for their explanation.

"Oh, she just fell," my mother said.

Yep, we were a tight family all right. We had colluded in covering the truth about my stepfather beating the crap out of me. I had some idea of the stakes involved when I lied, and although I certainly wanted my stepfather out of my life, I did not want to be taken from my mother. She never did anything to physically hurt me…and she was my mother. I didn't want to leave her home, I just wanted her to get rid of him.

The school staff bought our lies and sent me home for the day. It took much longer for the pain from my wounds to go away, but not one more word was spoken about what had happened. We just went on with our familiar roles and routines, only now I knew much more about how mean this "nice man" could be and the real dangers that I faced living under his roof.

It wasn't just that my stepfather was a constant threat to launch into another verbal or physical tirade. No, something else was beginning to emerge. After the school got involved in our business, my mother and stepfather were beginning to look at me as a source of potential trouble for them.

Meanwhile, my fighting spirit continued to rise up. More and more, when Jack taunted me I would shout right back in his face. Unfortunately, I also showed signs of mimicking his violent behavior. On more than one occasion while taking care of my little sister, I would yell at her, slap her, and one time I even held a knife to her while I had her pinned against the wall. In response to being terrorized by the bully that lived in our house, I was becoming more of a bully myself.

Oh, and I was still wetting the bed sometimes. Jack had taken me to a doctor for a medical evaluation at some point, but when they didn't give him the answer he wanted to hear, he took that as permission to keep taunting me for something that was entirely out of my control. One morning, after he had come home from the night shift and my mother had gone off to Pizza Caboose for her morning lunch-prep duties, he pulled back my blankets to see if I had wet the bed. The answer, as I knew, was yes.

"Get up!" he ordered. "Leave your underwear on. Just put your school clothes on over that. If you're going to live like an animal, you're going to go to school like an animal."

So I did. Now by fourth grade, the kids at my school were already used to teasing and taunting me for my appearance. My long hair was always full of ratty snarls because my mother had never taken the time to make sure I knew how to properly wash and brush it. I didn't bathe regularly, and my clothes were often dirty. Just like at home, I got used to being called names at school: Fatty. Stinky. Garbage Can. When I would walk by a group of the other kids, they would make "Bhew, bhew" vomiting sounds, and they loved to greet me with a little song that went, "Fatty, fatty, two by four, can't get through the kitchen door." So, when I arrived that morning, reeking from my urine-soaked underwear, they had one more reason to torment me. Now I was "Animal," just as Jack wanted me to be seen. I was sub-human.

Just like at home, I did not take the taunting at school sitting down. When they pushed my buttons, I would routinely throw the other kids' books across the room, or shove someone off his chair. After my blow-up, I would run out of class and get as far as I could before some teacher or school administrator tracked me down and reeled me back in. I served my share of detention and more than one suspension.

Only one teacher showed the ability to contain me. Mrs. Holycross, my Language Arts block teacher, just had a way of soothing me. She was a tiny woman with bright red hair that she set in curlers every night. She wore pencil skirts with a little jacket, and her pale face was highlighted by her crystal blue eyes and red lipstick. She could be strict as all get out, but I adored her. She was always fair to me. I remember one time when I got in trouble for something and she kept me back for recess. I didn't like that one bit, and after yelling my complaints to her I added emphasis to my point by spitting in her face.

"Okay," she said, barely flinching, "that just earned you another week of indoor recess."

During those recess detentions, she had me sit in her room. While she calmly read her book, I would quietly read my little books, too. Somehow Mrs. Holycross understood me, better than I could understand myself. Back then I could not have figured out that when the other kids goaded me, and then laughed when I took the bait and launched into my mini-rage, I was just acting out. I was desperately seeking the attention I never got at home, except for being tormented and beaten. Spending quiet, one-on-one time with Mrs. Holycross was just the kind of calm, caring attention I craved.

Unfortunately, Mrs. Holycross was not present with me at home. With no change in that environment in sight, I decided that I would run away. Learning my lesson from that time I ran off to the Lloyd Center in Portland, I was going to be much more strategic about it this time. I concluded that if I were going to live on my own, I needed money. I was working on that. I also needed a place to live, somewhere that didn't get locked up at night like the skating rink. That was easy: I would go live in the South Park Blocks, the 12-block public park area in downtown Portland that drew all kinds of people because of its statues and other works of art, along with its drinking water wells and lots and lots of grassy areas and big trees where anyone could find a little space to relax…or hide.

So I focused on raising funds for my getaway. Oregon had a bottle bill at that time, which meant that you could turn in soda cans and beer bottles for a nickel apiece. I took as many bottles as I could get my hands on to the local 7-Eleven and cashed them in. That was a solid start, but I was counting on a much bigger return from my participation in the March of Dimes Walkathon. Determined to walk the entire 20 miles, I took my sign-up sheet around and managed to gain a good number of pledges. Being Oregon, the conditions on Walkathon day were rainy and muddy. But I held up for the full 20 miles before coming home to sit in the bathtub, which was soon brown from the day's filth.

Then it was time to collect the money from my pledges. I believe you earned ten cents a mile for every mile walked, so I was going to build a pretty good-sized nest egg. The only trouble was, some people wanted to pay their pledge by check. "Oh, no, they only accept cash," I would argue. I fooled some of them, but others insisted that checks were indeed allowed and paid me that way. I put the checks away, thinking that I would figure out a way to cash them for myself someday, and I finished my round-up with a lot more cash than I had ever touched before.

I took my hard-earned money with me to school the next day. Going to school before running away was part of my plan because it would give me time before my parents figured out I was gone. Another part of my plan was to use some of that cash on Bubblicious Bubble Gum. I felt very proud of that idea: bubble gum was going to be all the food I needed. So, I stashed all the gum and the cash, along with the checks made out to the March of Dimes Walkathon, in a little tote bag. I tucked the bag in my school cubby after riding the bus to school. But while everyone was rushing off to first period class, I took my bag out of my cubby and walked right out the front door.

I reached the highway, crossed the street and sat down at the bus stop. I knew that I had to look for Bus Number 57: Portland. When the bus pulled up, I calmly got in, dropped my coins in the slot and found a seat. I knew that Portland was a long way away, but I wasn't sure how to know when we had gotten there. Finally, I decided to approach the bus driver.

Cray Cray

"When do we get to Portland?" I asked.

"Portland? Well, we just left Portland," he said.

"Oh, okay. Then can you tell me when we get back to Portland again?" He shook his head with a strange expression but said yes, and after going all the way out to Forest Grove, far west of the city, the bus, two hours later, finally came back to the point where the driver announced, "We're in Portland now."

After a brief walk, I recognized the Park Blocks from the days I used to go there with my father. I made it, I thought. Full of confidence, I promptly approached a rock wall where a bunch of people were talking to one another. I sat down and nonchalantly started chewing my gum, just taking my spot in this place where I belonged and would make my life. Of course, I was too young to realize that many of these people around me made their life in the park, too.

"So, what are you doing here?" one of the homeless women asked.

"Oh, I'm a runaway," I announced. She just nodded her head and, after introducing me to a few of her friends, she let me be. I was just sitting there smiling when a young guy who had not been part of the group made a beeline for me.

"Well, hello," he said. "My name is Ben. What's yours?"

"I'm Kristy," I said. "I'm a runaway."

"Well, if you're a runaway then you probably haven't had lunch yet today," he said in a friendly tone. "Do you want something to eat?"

I was going to tell him about the bubble gum, but instead I just nodded. He walked me across the street to Hamburger Mary's. "Would you like a hamburger?" he asked, and of course I responded, "Yeah, that sounds good." He ordered a burger and fries for me and for himself, and as we waited for our food to arrive he started asking me questions. He seemed like a nice man, so I told him the whole story: about the nickel bottles and the March of Dimes, and even the Bubblicious. Then I had an idea.

"Can you help me get to a bank?" I asked, pulling the March of Dimes Walkathon checks out of my tote bag. "I need to get these cashed."

"Hmm," said Ben. "I'm sorry to tell you that you'll never get those cashed because those are written out to the Walkathon."

My heart dropped. Part of my perfect plan had just been torpedoed.

"You know," he said while we were eating our burgers, "it gets very dangerous out there in the park, especially at night. You really shouldn't be hanging out there."

"Oh, where should I go then?" I asked innocently, expecting him to provide a vital tip for how to live happily as a runaway in Portland.

"Well, you know, the thing is you probably need to go home."

"Um, no, I'm not going home."

At that moment two police officers walked in and approached our table. My heart dropped into my stomach. Ben called the cops! These cops put me in little handcuffs and made me walk five blocks to their police cruiser. When they put me in the back, I was thinking, *oh no, I've got cigarettes on me and I'm going to get in big trouble!* By the age of ten, I had gotten used to stealing and smoking my mother's cigarettes. Even with everything else going on, all I could think of was that I just could not get caught with the cigarettes. I sneakily reached into my back pocket, pulled out the pack of Winstons and shoved them down inside the car seat.

I suppose the cops were trying to teach me a lesson but what they did next just seemed cruel. They drove to their precinct headquarters, parked their cruiser and told me they were going to have lunch and would be back in a while. They just left me, scared to death, in handcuffs, to wait and wait for them to return. When they did, they told me they had to take me somewhere else. When we approached the Donald E. Long Juvenile Detention Center, I recognized the place right away. My father used to drive by there when I was younger, probably after that first time I ran away to the mall. He would point and tell me, "If you don't straighten up, you're going to end up there someday." And now, here I was, sitting with my handcuffs and heading toward kids' jail.

I didn't get that far. After the adults made a big show of searching my little tote bag and processing me, my mother and stepfather arrived. I just had to promise "I'll be good, I won't run away again," and I would not have to go to jail. So I did what I had to do, and we all drove home. As usual, everyone was silent. As we went inside, my mother said, "Go eat your leftovers and get to bed."

For the rest of that night and the many days and nights to come, the silence just grew louder and louder. My mother neglected me, my stepfather beat me and tormented me, the kids at my school bullied me, and I had nowhere to run to. I may not have been in real jail, but it sure felt like it.

3

The Problem Child

I'm not sure when I began taking a greater interest in horses. It was probably around the time that I started regularly going to bed as soon as I came home from school. Sometimes I'd wake up late at night and watch Johnny Carson on *The Tonight Show* and linger in the dark living room a few hours longer. With Jack off at work, it was a rare peaceful time. I had outgrown my little girl escapes on the seat of that rusty old pickup, and now that I was on record as promising that I would not run away, I had to find new ways to ward off my deep loneliness.

I knew my mother loved horses. I still held that image of her arriving on the back of a horse, in the snow, at that place I was living with my father. What I didn't know then and would only find out many years later was that her grandmother, Millie, had an even stronger connection to horses. From what I was told, my great-grandmother was once a trick rider with the Pendleton Round-Up, a big-time rodeo held every September in Pendleton, Oregon. She would stand up on the saddle and do her little tricks to the delight of the many thousands of people who came from hundreds or even thousands of miles to see the big event. Part of the Pendleton Round-up is a major celebration of Native American people and traditions. The story passed on to me is that Millie herself was Native American. I met her only once when I was little, but I remember her black hair, brown eyes and dark skin. That part of the story may not prove to be true, but I know for sure that she and my great-grandfather Winn once owned Arabian horses.

So, as a girl of 10 or 11, I was feeling that family pull to go find myself a horse and ride it. When I came upon a pony being kept in the field of a farm owned by an old man not far from our house, I seized my opportunity. The horse looked lonely. I began by coming up close to his field and feeding him carrots and sugar cubes through the fence. He seemed to like me well enough. One day I heard the old man call the pony Ebenezer. From that day forward, I was determined that I would ride "Ebie" and that he and I would become the best of friends.

Recognizing that I needed to take certain steps to make that happen, I climbed on the ten-speed red, white and blue bike that my father had bought for me and headed for the feed store one day. Walking up the ramp to where they had all kinds of tack, I was a girl on a mission: get a pony bridle. When I found the one that seemed like the right size for Ebie, I immediately shoved it down my pants and walked out of the store. Back at home, I got my hands on a whole bunch of sugar cubes. Time to put my plan into action!

On my next visit, I stepped right into the field where Ebie roamed and used the sugar cubes to lure him into the barn so the old man wouldn't see us. Standing on a hay bale, I tried the bridle on him. It fit him perfectly and he took to it just fine. So far, so good. I didn't go any further that day, but I was soon coming over regularly, using apples from home along with the sugar cubes to coax him back into the barn. He was a Shetland pony, and I have to admit he wasn't all that nice. In fact, he bit me more than a few times. That didn't deter me, though. This was my pony and we were going to keep building our relationship.

The first time I climbed on his back, I held tight to the reins and Ebenezer's mane. "Don't buck me off, Ebie," I said softly. I guided him out of the barn, on the side not visible from the old man's house. When Ebie began trotting, I could tell that he was agitated with having me on his back. But he smoothed out quick enough, and I began riding him around as confident as any cowgirl prepping for a show.

I got bolder, coming over every day and stashing the bridle in a haystack in the barn. Then I began riding him off the field and into our neighborhood. When some of our neighbors greeted me with a suspicious look, I would just say, "Oh, he's mine." To justify the lie, and convince myself that it was somehow all right to be "borrowing" this old man's pony, I would say to myself, "Well, that man doesn't brush him and doesn't take care of him. *I'm* taking care of him. Ebie needs me."

I wasn't concerned about my mother and stepfather finding out about what I was doing because they were never around and didn't care. But it didn't take long for the old man to catch on to what was happening. He would walk out onto his porch with his cane, stand up and yell, "Get back here with my horse!" I just smiled and went right on riding.

Even if I had known then that this old man kept the pony just so his grandchildren could ride it when they visited him each summer, I'm not sure I would have stopped. This was my pony and he was going to do something very important for me in my life. All those kids at school who hated me? This pony would be my ticket to make friends. I had already heard one girl at school bragging about having a pony, and the other kids liked her. Now they were going to like me. When a new girl moved in two blocks from our home and started school in my class, I spotted the opening I had been waiting for. It helped that Diane happened to like horses herself. Since she didn't yet know of my reputation around school, she invited me to come to her house. Her bedroom was full of horse pictures and horse statues.

"I know all about horses," she bragged. "I know how to handle them, and how to ride them. I can even whinny like a horse."

"Oh, that's cool," I said, and waited for the right time for my follow-up.

"Hey, Diane, I have a pony," I added. "Would you like to come meet him?"

"Really? Yeah!" she blurted out.

I told her to meet me at the baseball field at Reedville Elementary

School, where we were both fourth graders, about an hour after school one day. She rode back to school on her bicycle, and I arrived at the field proudly riding on the back of my very own pony, Ebenezer. Diane immediately started petting him and making her horse noises.

"So, would you like to have a turn? Do you want to ride Ebie?" I asked, imagining that this gesture would not only cement our friendship but encourage her to start telling all the other kids how great I was. My life was about to be completely transformed!

"Yeah, I'd like that," Diane said.

It took her longer than I thought it should to get up on Ebie and get comfortable, but I wasn't worried. This girl knew all about horses, after all. Or did she? Ebie must not have thought so, because he took off on a dead run. Ten seconds later, he had dumped Diane on the field...but he was still running! I ran after my pony, screaming, "Come back, Ebie! Come back!"

But Ebie didn't stop or turn around. He ran right out onto the Tualatin Valley Highway, where a truck finally stopped him in his tracks. By the time I reached the scene, Ebenezer was gone. I screamed and cried, and the truck driver turned me away so I wouldn't get too close to the bloody form of my fallen pony.

A minute later, though, I had stopped screaming. I was no longer thinking about Ebie. Because of what happened, I had lost my new friend Diane, which meant that the other kids at school would go on teasing and tormenting me...forever. And it was *her* fault!

Without my pony to ride, I had to walk home. When I wasn't muttering curses about Diane, I was worrying about getting in trouble. This just might be the sort of thing to get Jack taking out his belt again, and the old man who owned Ebie might try to send me off to the Donald E. Long kids' jail.

Yet that's not the way it happened. My mother, stepfather and the man who used to own Ebie were inside our house having a little talk when I approached. Since they left the front door open, I stood on the bottom stair heading up to the porch and began my rocking and bouncing routine, trying to keep a sense of balance and rhythm so my world would not explode around me. Which I was sure was going to happen at any moment. Instead, there was some stern talk but no beating. And rather than facing severe consequences, I was granted a totally surprising opportunity.

"A friend of mine has a Welsh pony," my mother explained a week later. "She wants YOU to take care of it. She wants to give this pony to you."

"What? How? I mean, sure, I can do that," I said in disbelief.

It sounded like a good idea. My mother was apparently trying to teach me how to take responsibility, while also finding a way to satisfy my desire to connect with a horse. She was a horse lover; she understood. Unfortunately, the pony was going to be kept with my step-grandmother in Hillsboro, the town we used to live in when we had the house on the property of Jack's family lumber business. But by now we had moved to Aloha, which meant about a five-mile bike ride down a narrow two-lane street called Baseline. I would have to go there every day to feed and water this pony that was now supposed to be mine.

Before long, that five-mile bike ride, and ten-mile total commute, began to seem longer than driving to Russia. The truth was, I didn't always keep up my end of the bargain. I skipped some of my feeding and watering appointments. Anyway, this horse was ornery and had a mind of its own. We started getting calls from my step-grandmother that he had run off. We were able to track him down each time, like the day he wandered over to a construction site. The police had been called in, and when my mother and I came upon the site, the guys there were feeding my horse powdered donuts. I couldn't decide if it was funny or crazy, or both.

Still, the horse was mine and I was expected to take care of it. I would start each morning with good intentions, but then usually find someplace comfortable to park my bike along Baseline where I would sit and rest…and rest some more. Then it was time to go home or head off to school, and that beautiful Welsh pony was left waiting for its basic necessities and care.

I never heard exactly what happened, but somehow or other this pony's official ownership no longer had my name attached to it. Given a second chance for success in this world that pulled me in so strongly, I had failed miserably.

This got me thinking that maybe I was just what everyone said I was: a lazy, fat, smelly, lying little girl who was always doing something wrong. A bad kid.

Around this time, I turned to religion looking for answers about what was wrong with me and what I should do about it. To be clear, my family did not join any church. My mother wasn't much for religion, although she did love celebrating Christmas because it gave her a great excuse to stock the house full of yummy holiday treats. I remember giving her a decoupage one Christmas. My homemade gift highlighted a sweet picture of Mother Mary tenderly holding Baby Jesus as she looked down at her holy child. Looking back at it now, I would say I gave it to her not so much as a way to honor the spirit of Jesus' birth as to show her the image of how a mother is supposed to gaze upon and treat her child—like her oldest daughter, for example.

Yet, I did have a sincere interest in getting close to God. At that time, churches would send vans through neighborhoods like ours inviting potential church-goers young and old to accept a ride to their Sunday services. So I started checking out churches. I tried a Pentecostal church where I liked the energy but didn't like the condemnation of groups of people like homosexuals. When I switched to a Methodist Church, I hardly got the chance to see what it was all about before they caught me smoking behind the church and kicked me out.

I kept on looking. Whenever I showed up at some new church as a nine-or-ten-year-old girl, I was expected to shuttle off to Bible study or the children's version of the regular service. Unh-unh. Not for me. I wanted no part of that kids' stuff and made clear my determination to stay for the regular adult service. This was serious to me. In my own way, I was looking for answers to the big questions: What is life about?

Cray Cray

What am I about? Where is my place in this world? I was a seeker of spiritual connection, a nine-year-old having an existential crisis.

The big question I really wanted to figure out was this: Was I a mistake? Was that why I was such a bad kid? Did God make a mistake allowing me to be born? Was I not supposed to be here? Many nights at home, when I would wake up around Johnny Carson time after going to bed right after school, I would wonder about all this.

At church, however, all they seemed to keep talking about was how we were all born with sin and were still sinners. Well, I did believe that I was a sinner but I didn't see myself as being just like everybody else. I was *really* bad and I wanted to know why, and I needed direction on what to do with my life. Unfortunately, I concluded that going to all these churches was not going to help me make sense of that. Anyway, in churches full of families where kids came with their parents rather than showing up alone like me, they couldn't make much sense of me. I just wasn't going to find any comfort there.

When it was time for fifth grade, I still had to face the reality of being labeled and ridiculed at school. I had no clue how I was ever going to get along with my classmates at Reedville Elementary School. The teasing and taunting did not let up one bit and, when pushed into a corner, I remained ever ready to strike back.

In music class one day we were learning square dancing, which meant that everyone had to pick partners. When it came time for the girls to pick the boys, I turned to the boy I thought looked like the tamest one.

"I'm not going to dance with that *gross* girl," he said as he quickly backed away from me.

Before the others even had a chance to laugh, I grabbed this boy who dared to reject me and proceeded to beat the living crap out of him. My fury could not be contained in the small music class, so I dragged him out of the classroom and down the stairs onto the asphalt, still pummeling him the whole time, even with a teacher trying to yank me off him. After I got through with this poor kid, I believe he wound up in the hospital.

I got suspended for that little "outburst." My first day back at school after my suspension, the kids immediately upped the level of their taunts, with new material to call upon. I was now "Wild Girl" or "Crazy." I tried to steer clear of them, turning my attention to one boy who had once been kind to me and even now was choosing not to join in the verbal abuse.

"Would you play tetherball with me?" I asked him. Two seconds after he amazingly said yes, a girl charged up to me.

"Hey, that's my boyfriend," she insisted. "Keep your dirty hands off of him."

Well, she shouldn't have used that word "dirty." To show her the error of her ways, I punched her as hard as I could. Instantly the blood started pouring out of her mouth.

The next scenes that unfolded on the blacktop of Reedville Elementary and beyond are all jumbled in my mind. I remember running and running, my mind racing. *I'm crazy. I must be crazy. What is wrong with me? Why am I so wild? What are they going to do with me now?*

Like a spooked horse, I just kept darting left and right, forward and back, and the teachers couldn't rein me in. Even when I just stuck with the tetherball pole, spinning round and round, the adults were too afraid to come near me. At one point, I heard the voice of Mrs. Holycross from her second-floor window.

"Why don't you just calm down now, Kristy?" she said. "You can come on in and talk to me. You're going to be okay, you're not in trouble."

"No! No!" I shouted.

When she left the window, I figured she was coming downstairs to get me off that tetherball herself because she knew I wouldn't take a swing at her. I adored that woman. Still, I wasn't going to let her take me away. I let go of the pole and made a run for the huge rhododendron bushes at the front of the school. Diving down, I tried to bury myself in where no one could see me. And even if those teachers or administrators did spot me, they weren't going to get me out.

Cray Cray

Well, the school staff understood that they were no match for me and called for reinforcements. As the police cars pulled into the school parking lot, I said to myself, "No, no, no! They're going to bring me back to Donald E. Long, and this time they're going to keep me in jail." I knew that I would be blamed for everything and that no one would stand up for me. I was the bad girl.

The police soon locked in on my location. At least they were kind enough to let Mrs. Holycross be the one to come close enough to the bushes to convince me to come out. The cops did not arrest me and cart me off to juvenile jail, though. Instead, I was escorted back inside school, to the nurse's station, where I vaguely remember lying on the cot and falling asleep. More than likely, they had sedated me. When I woke up, I kept my eyes closed long enough to hear adult voices discussing what to do with me. When I picked out the words "Children's Services," I figured things had gotten very serious.

At home, where there never was much serious talking, I was sent to my room and climbed in bed. I could easily hear the yelling from down the hall. As usual, Jack's voice was the loudest.

"You let her get away with murder!" he shouted to my mother. "I know what needs to be done with her, and I'm going to do it!"

I imagined him already loosening his belt and reflexively wrapped my arms around my shoulders to ward off his anticipated blows.

"No!" my mother wailed. "That's not going to fix her. You heard what they said at school. Something is wrong with her."

Wow, my mother had actually stood up for me! The volume on the shouting gradually tapered down, and when I heard footsteps coming up the stairs I knew they were hers, not his. When she opened my door, she offered me a slice of pizza.

"Kristy," she said calmly, "do you still want to live with us?"

"Yes, I want to live with you," I answered without hesitation. "I just want you to get a divorce." It was my go-to argument, my only line of defense.

She chuckled. "Well, that's not going to happen," she said.

"But he's a terrible person. You *have* to divorce him. You *have* to get him out of the house!"

By that point, Jack's behavior had evolved beyond tormenting and abuse and had entered the zone of sexual inappropriateness. Noticing that I was already developing, he would pinch me around my breast area. The man was just cruel.

As I got more and more defiant with my mother, she just kept falling back to that same question: do you want to live with us? I don't even know what I answered, only that I figured it didn't matter what I said anyway.

After my blow-up at school, my fifth-grade school year was officially over. A few days after my expulsion, Mrs. Holycross arrived at our house in late afternoon bringing me school work. She kept that up, almost every day after school, for weeks.

Someone else showed up at the house: representatives from the Children's Services Division. They interviewed me about all the trouble I kept getting into, the trouble that was all my fault, and they also talked to my mother and stepfather. Did they ask questions about Jack beating me with his belt, or taunting me about my weight, my bed-wetting and everything else he could dredge up to use against me? Did they check into his drunken rages? Uh…no. Did they talk to my mother about her alcoholism? Her bulimia? Of course not. Did they go into the school and talk to the teachers and staff about how all the other kids relentlessly bullied me with their teasing and name-calling? Hell, no.

No, they were just there to gather evidence that would determine that I was officially emotionally disturbed. I was the "problem child" and the only question was what to do about *me*. The walls of my home were closing in on me and something bad was coming. I could just feel it.

4
Disorder in the Court

My mother delivered the news to me at the Pizza Caboose, her favorite place to get drunk and talk on and on about her problems and everything that was wrong with the world. Only this time she wasn't drunk, and the one problem she was discussing was…me.

"The decision has been made," she began. "You're going to move to the Christie School."

"What? Why are you sending me away?" I asked.

"Your behavior is out of control, Kristy. *You're* out of control. But they can help you there."

I could feel the tears welling up. *Don't cry*, I thought *Don't do it. Don't let her know how you feel.*

"Well…but…how long will I be gone?" I stammered. "Do I get to come back home?"

"We don't know how long," she said, her eyes looking over my shoulder, "but yes, you'll come back. Well, anyway…."

Cutting off any further discussion, she whipped out a piece of paper with a list of things I would need to move out of our house and into this school for emotionally disturbed girls.

"The good news is that we get to go shopping tomorrow," she said in her perky voice.

The next day my mother was steering a selection of a whole new wardrobe for me. After finding some pants that fit, she picked out my first bra, a pink bra. Holding it up stirred images of my stepfather making gross comments about the changes in my body. I was still a couple of months shy of my 12th birthday.

"You'll need a bunch of T-shirts," my mother said. A couple of the T-shirts she scooped up had words printed on them. My attention focused on one that had just a single word displayed across the front: "Notorious."

"What does that mean, notorious?" I asked.

"Well, uh, that just means...it means that you're well known for your behavior," she said with a big smile.

Yes, I'm a bad girl and everyone knows it. And now they're making me leave home because I'm so bad.

The night before I was going to be taken away, I kept having images, brutal and dark images, from a movie I had seen on television recently. *Born Innocent* tells the story of a 14-year-old girl named Christine who gets sent off to some kind of reform school after living with a father who beat her and a mother who just kept smoking cigarettes and pretending not to notice. In the reform school, which also served as a jail for kids, the other girls taunt and beat Christine. In the scene that everyone remembers, they take out a broomstick and rape her with it.

That's the kind of place I'm going to, I thought. *And that's what's going to happen to me!*

That scene from the movie took over my mind and would not let go, flaring up again and again as I tossed and turned in my bed. But when morning dawned and my mother came to get me up, I didn't cry. I didn't throw a tantrum, didn't scream that they couldn't take me there, that I didn't want to be raped like Christine. I made no move to try to run out of the house. No, I didn't say one word about that movie because I was convinced that any emotional display would just convince them that I was even more "disturbed." And then I would never be allowed to come home again.

Standing with my two little nylon tote bags filled with the pink bra and the "Notorious" T-shirt and all my other new clothes, I took one last look around my room. Practically everything else I owned would be staying right there. The white desk with gold trim that my father bought me wasn't going with me, and neither was the Lite-Brite with the colored plastic pegs that I spent hours making designs on. The posters from *Weekly Reader* of horses, kittens, whales and other fish and animals would be left hanging on my walls. On my bed lay Herbie, my big stuffed Lion that I got for Christmas when I was eight and was precious to me even though on that same Christmas Day I spilled hot chocolate on his face and cried when I couldn't wash it off. My Mickey Mouse Record Player, with Mickey's arm extending so caringly right to the turntable, remained in the corner. I would play and sing along to the Helen Reddy song "I Am Woman" over and over after I came home from school on that record player before drifting off to sleep to avoid my stepfather, not coming out until he had gone off to his night shift and it was safe to watch Johnny Carson in the living room.

"Hurry up, Kristy!" my mother called from that living room now. "We've got to get going."

I loved that room and I hated that room. At times, it had been my haven, my only safe refuge, but at other times it had been the place where Jack had beaten me or my mother tried to talk to me without ever offering me the love, understanding and protection that I needed. And yet, I didn't want to leave that room, or say goodbye to Herbie and all my other things. It was my home, and the only way I could cover my sadness about having it taken away from me was to tell myself that one day I would return.

Everything will still be here when I get back, just the way it is now, I thought. *And then things will be different. I won't be bad anymore and they will love me and want me with them.*

Dragging myself downstairs, my feet felt as if they were stuck in mud. Outside the bathroom, the last goodbye was the one that got to me. Maggie had been brought into our home as a hunting dog but in the last couple of years she really had become mine. She was a high-energy dog, and I would chase her all over heck and back, but she would keep my sister and I company many times when Jack and my mother were out at work or drinking or doing whatever they did that kept them away from us.

"You know that I love you," I told Maggie as I knelt and petted her chocolate head. "I have to go away now, but I'll be back. You be good while I'm gone now, girl. You just…"

The tears choked away any remaining words I meant to say. I could no longer pretend that this was anything other than the heaviest, saddest day of my life. *Stand up, don't let them know.*

"Let's go!" my stepfather shouted from outside. Closing the door, I slowly stepped toward our little coupe, in which I would need to squeeze in with my sister, mother and Jack. He grabbed my two bags, tossed them in the trunk and closed the lid with a thump. As the car pulled away, I did not look back.

We drove down York Street in Aloha and made our way onto the Tualatin Valley Highway, heading toward Portland. Christie School was south of the city, adjacent to Marylhurst College. As we entered the grounds, I was struck by how beautiful everything looked. It was all so lush and green, with trees supplying plenty of shade. I even spotted some horses in a nearby field. "Maybe it won't be so bad here after all," I said to myself.

The parting with my family at school was nothing like my emotional goodbye with Maggie at home. They didn't want me and were probably eager to get rid of me, to get back to a home where the oldest daughter would not be around to act up and cause trouble. I was somebody else's problem child now.

Cray Cray

The Christie School was old. I didn't know all the details when I was checked in on that February day in 1976, but I have since learned that the school dates all the way back to 1908. In its early years, the Catholic nuns took care of the orphan girls and boys that were brought there. By the 1950s, the Christie School had transitioned into a residential treatment program for girls with emotional and behavioral issues: aggression, abuse, depression and being a runaway threat. I guess they checked off all those boxes for me. Years later I would find a description, passed along from the Christie School to another facility, that explained my case this way:

> **"Kristy had problems being beyond parental control, inability to adjust to public school, conflicts with peers and younger sister, poor emotional control—tantrums, hitting, threatening, other behavioral problems—stealing, lying, running away."**

Yep, I was a bad girl. And now I was going to be living and going to school someplace where they could "help" me. The Sisters were still involved with the school's administration, but trained professionals were handling the hands-on work inside those dusty brick buildings. The facility included three residential cottages. Mine was Clark, the second wing of the three and the one that jutted out further than the others.

I don't remember much about my first contact with the staff, but I vividly recall being handed the small plastic container with a lid on it and my name clearly written on the front. I was told that this is where I would keep my "personal" items, which made no sense to me because my personal items like Herbie the lion, my Lite Brite and my Mickey Mouse Record Player were all back home in my bedroom. This container would just be the storage area for basic supplies such as toothbrush and toothpaste, soap and shampoo. Nothing special about any of that, and anyway we weren't even allowed to keep our personal containers in our rooms. We would have to come get them when it was time to use what was kept inside. The only thing of real value to me that would be kept in this container with my name on it was my cigarettes. I had been stealing my mother's cigarettes for quite a while by then, and when my mother and stepfather made me smoke my way through a whole pack almost non-stop so I would get sick and be discouraged from wanting to smoke again, I did get sick but I didn't stop smoking. And now, strange as it may sound today for a girl still 11 years old, I had my mother's permission to officially be allowed to smoke at this school that was going to help me.

From the beginning of my stay at Christie School, I made one very clear and firm decision: I was not going to stick around long. I noticed immediately that this was not a locked facility, which meant it was ideal for runaways, especially girls like me who already had some experience in that arena. The way I looked at the situation, if I could not live at home I was not going to live somewhere that was not home, not unless it was somewhere that I chose, someplace where I made the rules, where I was in charge of me.

On my first couple of attempts to run away, I barely made it off grounds. Then I got smart. I convinced a girl named Roxanne to run away with me, and since Roxanne was three years older than me, I figured she might know a thing or two that I hadn't picked up yet. We mapped out a plan for our escape, which would begin during smoke break when they let us sit outside the back door and did not watch over us very carefully as we huffed and puffed away.

As soon as we were sure that no staff was watching, Roxanne and I got up from the stoop outside the back door and took off. We ran up a hill, past the school administration building and another quarter mile all the way to the main road beyond the entrance. We just ran and ran as fast as we could, not even turning around to see if anyone was chasing us. With nothing but the clothes on our backs, we stuck out our thumbs to hitch a ride to Portland. Some man stopped and invited us to get in his car, and he didn't ask many questions on the ride all the way into the city.

I wasn't foolish enough to head back to the Park Blocks this time, knowing that the same blabbermouth or another one like him would be waiting to scoop us up and cart us off to the juvenile detention center or back to the Christie School. Roxanne had heard about a place called Arbuckle Flat, a hippie-type coffee house. We didn't know exactly what that meant, but we figured if there was any place where we might be comfortable hanging out, this was it. (Later I learned that it also housed a runaway center coordinated by the Portland Youth Advocates program and the Churches' Youth Ministry.) During the day, we slept in Arbuckle Flat's meditation room. In the evening, we'd try to blend in at the coffee house as late as we could, and then we'd just roam around inside or outside, wherever we believed that we wouldn't get caught, until they opened the doors and we could go back to the meditation room.

Our plan seemed to be working for the first day or two, but then one night we were approached by two guys wearing cutoff Levi jackets with a patch on the back and "Gypsy Joker" written on it. The Gypsy Joker Motorcycle Club used to be based in San Francisco but when they got into a little turf battle with the Hells Angels, they wound up relocating to Oregon.

"Hey, the police are about to raid Arbuckle. They're looking for runaways," one biker guy told me. "They'll find you here for sure. You've got to get out now!"

"What? Where should we go?" I asked.

"Don't worry, we'll take you out of here," he explained. "We're heading down to California right now. If you come with us, you won't get caught."

I was terrified, but I guess I believed him, and Roxanne did too, because we were soon hustling out the door toward their bikes.

"We'll need to split up," my biker guy said, motioning for Roxanne to get on the bike with the other Gypsy Joker. "That way we won't get caught. We'll rendezvous down the road later. Got to hurry now!"

And we were off. I have to admit, for a minute it felt like I had just embarked on a great adventure. But riding on the back of that motorcycle was cold, and scary, and I had time to realize I might be in danger. When we pulled into a rest stop, my biker said, "This is our meeting place. We'll wait for them here."

So, we waited and waited…and waited some more. As time dragged on, my sense of adventure gone, I grew more scared. *What am I doing with this biker guy? He could hurt me, even rape me! I've got to get away from him,* I thought. I just didn't know when it would be safe to make my move. After waiting three hours for his buddy and Roxanne to show up, my biker guy kicked up the bike, motioned for me to climb on and rode on for another two hours. By now, it had been dark forever. Pulling the bike into a ditch, he announced, "We need to sleep a few hours."

When he appeared close to dozing off, I made my move. Springing up from the ditch, I ran across the highway and began frantically waving at passing cars. Finally, a car with a couple in it stopped.

"I've run away and this biker guy…just take me to the police station!" I blurted out. The couple delivered me to the closest police station, and I didn't try to lie my way out of trouble when I got there. The cops contacted the Christie School to confirm my story, and after a long drive from somewhere in southern Oregon I was back "home."

"You're one lucky girl," the night attendant said. I never did see Roxanne that night or early the next morning. In fact, I never saw her again. I don't know what happened to her and could only hope she had found her way out of our adventure safely.

One day in February 1976, when I was still 11 years old, I was called to go on an outing to attend to official "business." By then I had been assigned to Cecily, a caseworker with the Washington County Children's Services office. When I climbed into her gold-covered Chevy Vega, she made me an offer.

"I'll let you smoke," she said, "but you have to promise you'll stay in the car and not try to run away."

When I nodded, she slid her pack of Merit cigarettes toward me.

"We're going to court today," she explained. "Your mother and father will both be there."

I had hardly seen my dad, except for those Sunday drives including the one that ended with him and my stepfather being carted off to jail in

Cray Cray

separate police cruisers. I wanted him to be there at court, wanted him to come barging in and declare that he loved me, that he would take me to live with him, that he would keep me safe from the stepfather that beat me. But I didn't believe that would happen. By then I was used to everyone in my life letting me down, and he hadn't exactly rushed in to try to stop my mother from taking me away in the first place. We drove for nearly an hour, mostly in silence, with Cecily occasionally asking me questions about the Christie School. I didn't say much about that, but I asked her what they would do in court.

"It's just something they need to do for you to stay at the Christie School longer," she said.

Stay longer! They're never going to let me out of there. I'm going to have to do something about that.

As best as I can remember it, the Washington County Courthouse in Hillsboro, the town where my mother had lived, was in the same building or adjacent building to the county jail. Cecily walked me down the hallway into a little room where my mother was already waiting.

"Where's Dad?" I asked right away.

"Oh, your father's not coming," she said. "He fell off a ladder at work and hurt his back."

I knew he wouldn't come!

I was getting angry and wanted to do something to show it, but I didn't know what yet. When my mother got called into the courtroom, I caught a glimpse inside. I could see the two tables, one for the defense and for the prosecution, just like real court. And I knew that whatever went on in that courtroom, it would end up with them just confirming how bad I was and how I had to be kept at the school for disturbed girls. I watched my mother head to the table where Cecily and someone I didn't know were already sitting. Then the door was closed to my little room, and someone from the court stood just inside it. *Wow, they know I'm a runaway risk,* I thought. *Just got to sit tight.*

The minutes passed. I just kept thinking about how they were talking about me in there and that they would decide I was so bad I would need to be punished. Maybe they wouldn't send me back to Christie School. Maybe they were going to send me someplace even worse. Courts had the power to do anything to you.

I began rocking in my chair and counting the tiles on the floor. They were big, square tiles, kind of a dingy yellow. *One, two, three, four...* When I got tired of the counting, and the rocking, I started tapping the wood grain table with the metal legs. The guard just watched me. Finally, Cecily opened the door and popped her head inside my little room.

"Okay, Kristy," she said in a kind voice. "We're ready for you now."

She escorted me to a chair by the side of a table. My mother and the others I didn't recognize were sitting behind the table with serious expressions. I looked out at the rest of the courtroom, noticing those little swingy doors that only reached up about waist high, leading toward the gallery. It was just like *Perry Mason* on TV. Then I turned toward the front of the court and looked at the judge. He just sat up there on his riser with his gray hair like he was a king.

This old judge does not even know me, and he's going to make decisions about where I'm going to live? He's going to decide what to do with me? Fuck that!

The judge had his head down and fussed with his glasses as he rustled through some papers, full of stuff about me. The bad girl. All of a sudden, he looked up from his papers and stared right at me.

"Well," he said, folding his hands in front of him on that big riser, "is there anything that you would like to say to the court?"

Is there anything that I want to say? Is he kidding? Like it really matters what I say, or what I think, or what I feel, or what I want! He has the power. He doesn't want to hear anything from me. He's already decided what they're going to do with me. They've all decided.

"Yeah, I'll tell you what I have to say to the court," I began, pretending to be calm. "Fuck you! Fuck you! That's what I have to say."

And with that, I bolted up from my chair, knocking it over, and ran

Cray Cray

through those doors I had come in through, then through another set of doors that opened to the hallway.

"Go get her!" the judge yelled.

As I raced down the hallway, I noticed a pay phone on the wall. Instantly I knew what I had to do. I jumped up on the wall, grabbed hold of that phone, and yanked with all my strength. I had torn it partly off its hinges when the court guy grabbed me. He wrapped his arms around my waist and tried to pull me away from the phone. Well, I was not going to let him win that easy. I was sick and tired of adults making me do things I didn't want to do, and trying to stop me from doing things that I wanted to do. I just tightened my grip on that phone dangling from its station on the wall. *No, no, no, you're not going to pull me down.*

And he didn't, well, not alone anyway. But when a second court guy came running up and started to peel my hands off the phone, while the first guy held me tightly by the waist, I lost my leverage. At first one of my arms dropped, then the other. I was a strong and feisty girl, but up against two well-conditioned men, I had met my match.

"You need to calm down now," the first guy said as I lay on the floor with him crouched over me, holding my wrists. I actually was calm, that is I was calmly assessing in my mind how I could get away now. I thought and I thought and…I could not see a way. I was defeated. These burly guys, and the old judge, and the strangers in the courtroom, and my parents who didn't care and didn't want me, they had all won. For now.

The two guys marched me back to the same waiting area where I had been rocking my chair, counting the tiles and tapping the desk. Cecily came in.

"Well, it's done," she said. "We're going to go now."

She tried to explain the court decision, and although I could not have articulated it exactly at the time, I had just been made a ward of the state. The state of Oregon would be my official guardian now. It would decide what to do with me. My parents had given me up. Many years later, I found the official court document:

February 18th 1976

In the Circuit Court of the State of Oregon for the County of Washington Juvenile Department

Kristy Sue (last name withheld for confidentiality) is within the jurisdiction of the Court by reason of the following facts: The behavior, condition and circumstances of said child are such to endanger her own welfare by reason of the following facts: Said child has been expelled from Reedville Elementary School for physical and verbal assaults on students and school personnel; she does not obey her parents' rules and regulations; she has emotional problems and needs residential treatment.

"We're going back to the Christie School," Cecily said as we approached her gold Vega. "Can I take you there by myself? You won't run away, will you?" I shook my head, but Cecily still seemed a little nervous. "No, I'm not running anywhere," I added. That seemed to convince her. Anyway, I think she could see that I was heartbroken. My parents—my mother, really, since she had sole custody—had given me away. Like Cecily said, it's done.

I didn't blame Cecily. I actually kind of liked her. She wasn't old like that judge, maybe in her 30s, and she was a slender woman, with red curly hair and a long face. She was always steady with me, never raised her voice, didn't try to lecture me. No, this was not Cecily's fault.

I sat in the passenger seat with my legs pulled up, crisscrossed, and blew out the smoke from one of Cecily's Merits as I let the wind blow back my hair through the open window. Cecily's red hair was blowing too.

"We just smoked the last of my cigarettes," she said as she pulled into the parking lot of a convenience store. She smiled and then added, "So, can I go inside by myself and trust you here alone in the car?"

"Yes, you can trust me," I said softly. And I meant it, too. I was a person of my word—with Cecily at least.

I settled back into the routine at the Christie School. I was the youngest

Cray Cray

girl there. Most of the others were 13, 14, 15, even 16. The "school" part of Christie School life was difficult for me, not just because I was younger but because I had missed almost the entire fifth grade after they expelled me for my little tantrum. A lot of what they tried to teach me in the Christie classroom went right over my head.

In the community, though, I was determined not to let my age hold me down. I tested the rules and limits often, and I was held accountable. More than once, sometimes daily, I was taken down by staff. But after the court ruling I was mostly just biding my time with the staff, and among the other girls I was not going to be content with just keeping up. I would become the leader! I had my next plan in my head for a while before I started sharing it with the girls I trusted.

"Look, I got caught that last time because there were only two of us," I said. "But if we all run away together, they'll never catch us! We need to have a mass runaway."

Good ideas have a way of catching on, especially in a school for emotionally troubled girls who feel held down, abandoned, lost, unloved. Why should any of us want to stay there? Why wouldn't we all want to be free?

I kept count of the "yes" responses, and once I got up to eight, I decided that we were ready for breakout day. It had been at least a couple of months since Roxanne and I snuck away during a smoke break outside the back door, and the staff had allowed us to resume our little routine. So, one Friday afternoon, the eight of us were down at the end of the hallway, just outside the open door, having our smoke break. One of the girls in my little pack had done some pre-trip "shopping." She had broken into the closet where they kept the cigarettes and had scored at least two cartons. That ought to keep us going for a while, I figured.

Making our initial getaway was ridiculously easy. When we got through the grounds, I directed my pack to split up into two groups of four so we wouldn't look so...well, like what we were. We planned to meet up at a familiar park on the route heading toward Portland. From there, we'd decide how to proceed. We walked and walked, and hitchhiked for part of the way, and well before dark we had succeeded in meeting up at the target location. So far, so good.

"So now what, Kristy?" one of the girls asked me in the park.

Well, the truth was I didn't really have a concrete strategy for what to do next. Stalling for time, I pointed out that it was a nice evening and suggested that we should just enjoy the park for a while. It helped that we soon ran into a group of teenage boys, which worked to hold the other girls' interest.

"We ran away from this school we live at," I bragged to one of the boys. It didn't once occur to me that I might have been blowing our cover. The boys, being the chivalrous type, pledged to help us out. Since it appeared that we would need to spend the night in the park before making our next move, and since it was already getting very cold by the river, even before dark, they told us they were going home to get us some sleeping bags to keep warm.

"Great idea," I said, "and we can all just sleep in the girls' bathroom. That will be a perfect shelter."

So, the eight of us huddled in the bathroom and waited for the boys to get back with our bedding. And we waited some more. Finally, the restroom door flung open. But instead of the boys with our sleeping bags, the person who stepped inside was a female police officer. And she wasn't carrying any blankets or fluffy pillows to make our night warm and cozy.

"Let's see here, we've got one, two, three, four," she began, and when she got all the way up to eight, she nodded her head.

"So, girls, we can go easy or we can go hard," she went on. "Personally, I would suggest you go easy. Just wait right here until we get ready to take you out of here."

I was really angry. I was in charge of our group, and I was convinced that we had a clear path to freedom. We would have made it, too, if it wasn't for those boys. We should never have trusted them.

Cray Cray

We didn't resist, which I guess meant that we were choosing the easy way, and she and the other officers who suddenly showed up walked us out of that bathroom one by one. As they proceeded to put us in handcuffs, my mouth dropped open when I saw where they were escorting us: a police paddy wagon! They were taking a bunch of teenage girls, with me as the lone pre-teen, off to the police station in a freaking paddy wagon. *I wonder if they'll give us something to eat there*, I thought, and I did my best to hide how scared I felt to the other girls.

The Lake Oswego police station was tiny, with just three or four little holding cells. It was much smaller than the Juvenile Detention center I had wound up in after getting caught trying to live in the Portland Park Blocks that time. I was wondering what they were going to do with all of us there, and as I watched the police officers, I got the impression they were wondering the same thing. What do you do with a bunch of young girls at an adult jail? We could hear one of the policemen on the phone with an administrator at Christie School.

"But we have to bring them back there," he argued. "We can't keep them here…I don't care if you don't want them back, we're going to bring them back anyway. And we're leaving right now."

We were herded back into the same paddy wagon and 15 minutes later we were heading down the hill of the Christie School grounds toward the cottages. From the paddy wagon's headlights, we could see two staff people waiting for our arrival. One of the girls in our gang had a watch and said it was now two o'clock in the morning. The staff people were not looking very happy to see us. At least they gave us a snack before pointing us back to our rooms. I figured the stern lecture and punishment would come in the morning. I was wrong.

"Don't get too comfortable in there," said the woman who came to my room. "You're not staying."

"What…why? What do you mean I'm not staying? Where…where am I going?" I insisted.

"Portland. The police are taking you to the Donald E. Long home," she said.

Jail? I'm going back to jail, not the little jail in Lake Oswego but the big jail I saw that other time? Oh no, no, no, I'm not coming back from one jail at 2 in the morning just to be told I'm going to some other jail.

It took two staff people to corral me and get me outside. There, in the glare of flashing police lights, I noted that a different police department, maybe the county, had been rushed to the scene, and that two of my pack members had also been pulled out of school to be whisked off to jail. I did not like this, did not like it one bit. I was their leader.

They had a van waiting to transport us, and as I broke free from the Christie School staffers I jumped right in front of it.

"No! You can't take us!" I screamed. Kicking my feet out to ward off the advancing policemen, I climbed on top of the van and, in a repeat performance of yanking part of the pay phone from the wall at court, I started pulling on the windshield wipers. I couldn't get them off, but I did a pretty good job of bending them.

That must have made the cops mad, because one officer climbed up on the hood of the van with me and picked me up by the neck, like a puppy that had busted into a chicken coop. He gripped me tight, then a little tighter, and the next thing I knew I was out. Cold. Unconscious. Me, a pre-adolescent girl just trying to express my displeasure at how I was being treated by a bunch of adults who didn't understand and had total control over my life.

I was out for a minute or two, or maybe four or five, and when I came to, I witnessed a sight that in the moment filled me with a sense of pride. Dozens of the other girls had come pouring out of the cottages and were yelling and screaming at the Christie staff and the cops. I had started a riot! Yep, I was still the ringleader of the emotionally troubled girls of Christie School, and in my young mind my achievement that night was something to wear like a badge of honor. Like the bad boy stereotype in the movie *The Breakfast Club*, I was the girl "bad boy" of our gang.

So that final scene at Christie School felt like something of a triumph in that moment, but, of course, it didn't mean that I had won. The police finally did stuff me into the back of a police cruiser reserved just for me, and even as Jill, one of the nicer staff members, tried to reassure me that "you can come back, you just need a break," I knew better. As the police whisked me away to the Donald E. Long Juvenile Detention Center, I was going to jail. And I realized that this time, I was not going to be leaving after a few words of warning and a solemn promise to be better. I was busted.

The bad girl had become the biggest bad-ass around.

5

A Star Still Shines

In the back of the policer cruiser on the long ride to the Donald E. Long Juvenile Detention Center, the bold and sassy badass ringleader of the riot that rocked the night at the Christie School melted into a wet pile of little-girl tears.

"What have I done?" I asked myself. "I can't stay at this school anymore. It really wasn't so bad there. Some of the staff even liked me. I blew it! Now I'm going to jail, that big, scary looking jail, and I don't know when they'll let me out of there or where they'll send me next. What's going to happen to me?"

I had a lot of time to think about these questions inside Donald E. Long. They placed me in isolation. "It's for your own protection," I was told, and it was true that the facility was full of girls much bigger and older than me and I might get hurt around them. I remember what those older girls had done to Christine in that movie *Born Innocent*. From the safe confines of my little cell, I could hear the others yelling at each other, their voices rising louder and louder, interspersed with lots of banging, thumping and whimpering. It seemed like a violent place.

So I spent hours and hours in my cell, with its pale institutional blue walls, a window protected by a heavy mesh screen, a single bed and no bathroom or toilet. I turned to my trusted routines to try to stay calm. It's what adult professionals would call "self-stimming," where a person in an environment with no natural stimulation, struggling with fear or anxiety, creates their own ways to stimulate themselves. The only problem was, in my empty room there wasn't much stimulus to call upon. Crouched on the floor, I resorted to lightly tapping my head against the wall. And, of course, I counted the number of times my head made contact with the hard surface.

They didn't leave me alone all day and night. When staff would come in with my meals, they would stay and talk with me while I ate. But most of the time, it was just me and my head tapping and my counting, and waiting and wondering and worrying…

Looking at that little girl, frightened and alone in a tiny room of juvenile jail in the summer of 1976, from the lens of today, I understand so much of what she could not put into words back then. My raging, those outbursts in court and among the flashing red lights of police in the dead of night, were triggered by my anger at my circumstance in life. I had been living in a family environment where my mother suffered from depression, bulimia, and alcoholism, my father had slipped far into the background of my upbringing, and my stepfather constantly belittled me and often added physical harm to his verbal abuse. And yet, rather than having the spotlight shined on their severe emotional and psychological problems, and the lack of love, caring, compassion, security and positive attention in my life, the spotlight was pointed on me. I was the problem. I was rejected, labeled and sent away to be fixed in environments that only served to reinforce my identity as the "bad girl." Now I had wound up in jail, a brutal place for any child, even if it's a "kids' jail."

My acting out was actually trying to make a statement: "Look at me. Listen to me. Something is seriously wrong with this picture of the way my life is going. This is not the way it's supposed to be, and somebody needs to wake up and see what's happening and do something about it." Feeling unseen and unheard, it was like I was invisible. That's why I found ways to behave in which I would become visible. I desperately needed someone to understand the pain I was in. Then, somehow, others would step in and rearrange that picture of my life. Someone would regard me not as a horrible and hopeless bad girl, but as a beautiful but wounded child, totally worthy of love and understanding. I needed an angel, or better yet, an army of angels.

And every so often, one would show up and, for a moment or two anyway, soothe my suffering and leave behind a kernel of hope. Through a kind gesture or nurturing words, they would remind me that love and caring were still out there.

One of those angels worked the evening shift at Donald E. Long. I didn't see her during my first few days in jail, but one evening she came in with a sweet smile holding out a bottle of Pepsi Lite for me. It was well after dinner, so I was not scheduled to receive any more food or drink. But it was summer time, and my cell was extremely hot, and this woman knew just what I needed. I can still remember the extreme sensation of cold when I held that bottle up to my face. Never have I so appreciated a simple bottle of soda.

She brought her own drink, too, and she was also carrying some magazines. She was obviously planning to stay awhile. When she sat down, she offered me my choice from the age-appropriate magazines in her pile. We sat and drank and read. She didn't say much, but she didn't need to. Her gesture said it all: "I care about you, you're a human being, not a monster, you're not alone, it's going to be all right." And the best thing about this evening visit was that it did not turn out to be a one-time deal. Night after night she would show up in my room, her hands full of magazines and Pepsi Lite. She would leave my magazines behind, and for hours I would reread them over and over again because doing so reminded me of this sweet lady.

Bolstered by this simple but loving gesture, my moments of despair while alone in my cell were at least balanced by moments when I believed that maybe things really could be all right. I just didn't know how or when.

Eventually, they began letting me out of my "room" for meals with the general population. It was good to break free from isolation, but scary. A staff person had to be seated at every table to head off any potential fights among girls armed with knives and forks. Oh, and they were constantly counting all that silverware, too.

I don't remember my mom and stepfather visiting me all this time, but, ironically, I did have a pleasant experience when my stepfather's mother came to see me. She brought me some cannoli and we were allowed to eat it together in the visiting room.

After six weeks in juvenile detention, the waiting and wondering finally came to an end. I was escorted out for what was called a "staffing," which meant a meeting of Donald E. Long staff and other adults who would be discussing my situation. In other words, I would learn what they were going to do with me next. I wasn't so afraid of what would happen this time, because whatever it was could not be worse than living in jail. Even as a 12-year-old, I knew that jail is no place for any child.

This time, rather than a courtroom, the adults were gathered in a large circle around a conference table. My mother was there, but not my father—again. Cecily had a seat at the table, and so did a couple of staff members from the Christie School. Just as it was that time in court, I didn't recognize the others. One of the strangers came up to me and introduced himself as Peter Williamson.

"We're all going to meet here together for a few moments, then you and I are going to meet alone," he explained. "Then the whole team will come back together. Okay?"

I just shrugged. Once again, I knew that I would not be having any input into any decision to be made about my life anyway. I was just a ward of the state. Nothing much happened until I found myself alone in a separate room with this Peter Williamson, a short man with glasses and a little goatee.

"Have a seat," he said. As soon as he sat down, he reached into a pile of papers in front of him and started balling up the first piece. I just looked at him, and he looked at me. What on earth is he doing with that paper? I thought. After crinkling up a few more pieces of paper, he took the first ball of paper and tossed it at me. He didn't throw it fast or hard, but it was clearly directed right at me. Then he threw another ball and another one.

"Is there something he wants me to do?" I asked myself, and then I got it. He was trying to provoke me, to get me mad, to fly into another of my famous fits of rage, which no doubt would be used as further ammunition to put me away somewhere horrible for a long time. Ha!

"Are you freaking kidding me?" I said to myself. "This is so stupid. You know what, buddy? I'm not going to bite." He finally gave up, and we sat and talked for a while. Eventually he must have decided he had whatever "evidence" he needed because he motioned for me to get up and began walking me back toward the conference room. From the lobby area outside that room, I could see out a window. I noticed the Christie School van parked there. Mr. Williamson pointed to a chair and told me to have a seat. The door to the conference room was open, and my mother had a direct view of me sitting down on that chair.

"You aren't leaving her out there alone, are you?" she asked Mr. Williamson.

"She'll be fine," he said, and then he closed the door.

That's what he thinks! He should have listened to my mother, she knows me.

I got up from my chair and went to the bathroom. "What's the plan here?" I asked myself, shifting into my badass persona like Clark Kent slipping into the phone booth to don his Superman outfit. "I need a plan and a way to execute it."

In a flash, I thought of the two Christie School staff members in the conference room and their van parked outside. *That's it! I can arrange a little ride back to Christie School with them. They'll never know the difference...*

Leaving the bathroom, I hustled to the door outside, scooted to the parking lot and located the Christie School cargo van with three benches in the back. Without a moment's hesitation, I climbed in and scrunched under the bench furthest back. And then I waited. When the front doors opened and the two women got in, I barely let myself breathe.

"I guess Kristy ran away again," one of them said. "She sure is a master runaway."

"Well, they're catch her soon, I'm sure," the other said. "Hope she'll be okay."

And then they shifted into talking about school and their lives and things I didn't understand except that it had nothing to do with me. Which meant that my plan was working, and my hiding place was secure. *As soon as they get back to Christie School, I'll just give them enough time to walk away out of sight, and then I'll pop up out of here. Then I'll hitch a ride to Portland, and I'll know what do there. This is all going to work. I'm going to get away!*

After we arrived at school, and waiting an extra minute to make sure they were long gone, I squeezed my way out of my secret perch. Then I climbed over the seat and, as quietly as I could, I opened the side door. Surprise!

"Well, hello," the van driver said. "And where do you think you're going, young lady?"

I was furious. How could they have known? I was the quietest little church mouse back there.

With nowhere to run, I relented to being driven back to Donald E. Long. I got processed all over again and handcuffed to a bench while they decided where they were going to put me and whatever else they had to work out. All I could think about was how hungry I was getting. It seemed like every time I ran away, I would wind up going hours and hours without a meal. This is so unfair! I thought. Finally, I wound up back in the same isolation cell. I didn't see the sweet lady with the Pepsi Lite and the magazines again, but I was only there for a few days when they took me out and told me I was going to some hospital.

It was a stranger, not Cecily, who drove me this time, but he also happened to smoke Merit cigarettes and when I asked him for a smoke he begrudgingly handed me one. When we got to the hospital, my mother was already seated in a small office. I understood that it had something to do with financial arrangements.

Cray Cray

"Everything's going to be okay," she said to me. I looked at her closely, which I couldn't even bear to do when I saw her in that conference room. With her olive skin, brown eyes and black hair, she still looked beautiful to me. After everything that had happened, I still loved her and still clung to that little girl hope that somehow, someday, she would love me enough to want to take me home and make a commitment to love me and care for me.

"They'll take good care of you here," she added, and that snapped me out of it. It was the same message, with the same reassuring tone, she had tried to give me when she was sending me off to Christie School more than six months earlier. She didn't want me home. Anyway, I belonged to the state, and Cedar Hills Hospital in Portland is where the state had ruled I should live now. At least I wasn't in jail.

Over time, I learned a bit more about this latest intervention. Apparently, my parents had an excellent medical insurance policy. It would cover a stay at this private psychiatric hospital for some period of time. And in this kind of environment, I would be treated professionally as a patient, not as a girl who just needed to live and attend school somewhere that emotionally troubled girls could be accommodated.

The problem was that none of these other patients happened to be 12-year-old girls. There were a handful of teenagers, girls who were all older than me, but otherwise the population was filled with adults. And many of these adults had some serious problems, displaying behavior several notches above my little childish outbursts.

My roommate, who I believed had recently turned 18, was placed in this hospital after watching her fiancé die in a terrible accident that she had witnessed. She did not speak and hardly moved—totally catatonic. On my third or fourth day at Cedar Hills Hospital, a woman who was admitted and stripped of all her clothes in preparation to be dressed in a hospital gown squirmed away and began turning cartwheels, nude, all the way down the hallway. The staff called a code. With her screaming and flailing her arms, it took three of them jumping on her to finally subdue this new patient. I watched for a minute or two from my room before closing my door and turning back to my radio.

Another time I saw a woman smearing her own feces all over herself. She even put some to her mouth. I witnessed another patient just after she had stabbed herself with a razor. As blood pooled on the floor around her, I covered my eyes, flashing back to the day I watched my mother cutting herself with a knife in our bathroom. Sometimes patients would be dragged off to seclusion after some big blow-up and would never be seen again, at least not on our little ward.

A few patients would often focus their steely-eyed attention on me, probably because I was the "little girl" of the group. One woman, old enough to be my mother, began to believe that this was actually who she was to me. "Katie, my dear child," she would say as she reached out to touch me. I don't know whether Katie was her daughter's name or what, but I would back away from her advances as fast as I could. At least she looked at me with something that could almost be called affection, unlike the patient who would point at me and scream, "It's her! It's her. She is the one who's doing it. She knows!" What it was that I was supposedly doing, and what I knew, I was far too scared to find out. Being around these patients, I was convinced that one day one of them would get me alone in some corner and that would be the end of me.

I guess I was pegged as someone who was heading in the direction of these psychotic patients because when I was admitted, I began on the highest level of security. That meant an initial 24-hour observation period. Like that woman I later saw doing naked cartwheels in the hall, I was stripped down and given a hospital gown. Then I was placed on a mattress where I would be watched, like an animal just assigned to a zoo, assessed for potential dangerous behavior.

I guess I passed their test because I was allowed to take my place among the crazed women. Living in a psychiatric hospital, my basic treatment included being medicated. This was my first experience with any kind of anti-psychotic medication, and it made a real impression on me. I was put on Thorazine and even though it was probably a low dosage since I was a child, I soon found it so hard to move my body that I felt like

Cray Cray

I was walking in quicksand. The drug also made me lethargic, which led to an almost immediate weight gain, and it generally distorted my perceptions so much that I began to feel like I was walking around in a fun house. As I would learn later, Thorazine is a pretty heavy-duty drug for a little kid. I'm pretty sure I was also on an antidepressant, though I don't remember what it was. Looking back, I could agree that I was depressive and could benefit from an antidepressant, but to be given an anti-psychotic drug? I was definitely not psychotic, just a girl prone to aggressive but creative bursts of anger as a way to be seen and heard for the pain she was in.

Oh, but they were working on those anger issues, all right. In the name of curing me of the impulses that led to my destructive behavior, they put me through this little routine that would begin as soon as a staff member came in to get me up in the morning. "Now, make your bed," she would say. Then, after standing there with a stern expression as she watched me tuck in my sheets and pull up the blanket, she would swoop in and rip the sheets off the bed. "Now make it again," she would command. Well, like the guy crumpling balls of paper and throwing them at me, she was not going to make me bite. I was not going to have a fit, even when she asked me to make my bed ten times.

Another part of my treatment plan was conducted in a patient room with nothing in it except two chairs and a little table. After I had been seated at one of the chairs, a staff woman would bring in a huge container of different-colored wooden beads. Then she would set up several small buckets, each labeled a different color. "Now sort all those beads by their different colors," she would say. So, while the staff person stepped outside the room and waited in the hallway, I dutifully began to start putting all the green ones in the green bucket and the red ones in the red bucket and the blue ones in the blue bucket. This is fucking stupid, I thought as I tried to contain my anger. But I did not do what they apparently expected me to do, which was to pick up all the little colored buckets and the huge container of beads and hurl them against the wall, or toward their heads. *They're not going to make me do it!* I thought. But just before I had completed the task and sorted each and every bead, the woman stepped back into the room, walked silently to the table and proceeded to pick up each and every bucket of beads and dump them back out.

"Now sort them again," she would say as she abruptly turned to walk back to the hallway. Although I didn't lash out in anger, which I was convinced she was hoping I would do, I did begin to concoct a way to ease my burden. When I was sure that she could not see me, I would take piles of beads into the bathroom and carefully flush them down the toilet. When she came back, expecting me to be about three-quarters of the way toward completion of my task, she was surprised to see that I had already sorted "all" the beads. I guess she decided that I had just learned how to get faster at separating the colors. Of course, she still went through with the next step of the treatment, which was to dump the beads out and direct me to resume sorting them again.

After my sixth or seventh round of sorting those damn beads, I began crying. "What do you want from me?" I asked. Noting that she had succeeded in breaking down my spirits, she pronounced the exercise "over" and scurried off to write her little comments in my record. And the next morning, one of her accomplices would show up in the early morning, rouse me out of bed, take me back to the same room, bring in the beads and the buckets and walk me through the same paces all over again, like a lion in training.

Oh, but I was highly motivated to act like a well-behaved lion. I understood that if I started yelling, screaming and knocking over tables, or pushing or shoving my "trainers," they would use that as further evidence of how bad and dangerous I was, how crazy I had become. And they made it clear that if I was clinically determined to be truly crazy, my next stop would be Oregon State Hospital. And if I thought things were strange and scary here at Cedar Hills, just wait until I got plucked up and deposited in the loony bin.

It was the constant threat held above my head, like a dangling sword. I wanted to avoid that terrible fate, and I didn't believe they should ever have to send me there anyway, but the reality was that during this impressionable time in life when a child begins to form the identity she will carry toward adulthood, I was beginning to wear the label of "mental patient." Living in a locked unit, taking anti-psychotic medication, being treated as a crazed animal capable of flying into a rage at the smallest provocation—it was all having an effect on me.

And the truth was, I did not always keep my behavior totally in check. Sometimes I caused enough trouble to have privileges taken away, and I even had to be restrained a couple of times. Of course, in my mind, the things I did were just pranks. I was, after all, still a kid. Sometimes I would just act that way, like that time I thought it would be funny to take the light bulbs out of every lamp in every patient's room when those patients were not there. I also grabbed as many of their pillows as I could, and then I stashed everything in a large enclosed shower. With a satisfied grin, I waited to see the staff's response, which was mostly losing some privileges and having my deed recorded in their little notes. Another time, after I had been denied going on a patient outing as punishment for something I had done on a previous outing, I walked out on the patio, grabbed an aluminum chair, climbed up on a cinderblock and put the chair down on the roof. That seemed like so much fun, I took all the patio furniture and moved it onto the roof. Whether the staff laughed or got ticked off when they returned and saw my handiwork didn't matter to me. I just wanted to get a reaction. I was still that girl needing to be seen.

From my first days at Cedar Hills, I really liked Richard, the recreational therapist. He was always fun to be around, and I could tell that he liked me. I was thrilled when I was one of the patients he selected to go on an outing to Portland Civic Auditorium to see the disco group KC and the Sunshine Band, a hot act in those days with songs such as "That's the Way (I Like It)," "(Shake, Shake, Shake) Shake Your Booty," and "Get Down Tonight."

I was having a fantastic time at the concert, and when I was out in the lobby unsupervised during intermission, I noticed a large display of glasses filled with wine on a counter. Thinking they were free, I quickly grabbed two. Moving swiftly, but careful not to spill a single drop, I hustled to the lady's room and chugged those two glasses of wine as fast as I could before anyone would notice what I was up to. Then I scooted back to my seat, which, since I liked Richard so much, happened to be the one right beside him. Trying not to vomit, I put my head between my knees; Richard noticed right away.

"Kristy, what's the matter? Are you okay?" he asked.

Oh, nothing was wrong with me, except that my head was spinning, I felt like I had just stepped out of a scalding fire, I was fighting the impulse to throw up and I reeked of alcohol.

"Oh my God," he said softly as he took a closer look at the evidence. He placed his hand on my back and looked at me with what appeared to be a mix of disappointment, concern…and maybe a kernel of understanding. "Just sit still," he said. "This will pass."

It was nice of Richard to keep a watch on me for the entire second act, but I was still miserable. In those days, I was smoking cigarettes regularly and I even had progressed to marijuana a few times, but I had never been intoxicated before. And from that night forward, when I would do many harmful things to my body, I never cared much for alcohol.

"So, here's what I've decided," Richard said when we got back to Cedar Hills late that night. "Your punishment for what you did at the concert will be not being allowed to go on the next outing. And we will never speak about this again. Understood?"

I nodded. As far as I know, he never reported my behavior, which was certainly good for me. I would imagine that avoiding any official mention of a 12-year-old patient getting drunk while on his watch was good for Richard, too. From that night on, I liked Richard even more.

As I mentioned, I had already been exposed to marijuana. I owe that opportunity to Sylvia, a patient who reminded me of my mother because she happened to be anorexic. Sylvia was apparently in much better psychological shape than most of the other adult patients, because she was allowed frequent passes. Each time she ventured into the outside world, she managed to get her hands on some weed. Since she kind of liked me, she was nice enough to share. I wasn't foolish enough to smoke a joint in the hospital, but I found another way. After I had been a patient for a while, and had proven myself to be mostly reliable, my psychiatrist, Dr. Deeny, began writing me afternoon passes to leave for an hour or so to go to the nearby shopping center. When I was out, I didn't do much shopping. I was too busy finding private nooks and crannies to smoke Sylvia's marijuana.

Dr. Deeny was a kind man who was always gentle with me. I believed he really did have my best interests at heart. Of course, I didn't like that he wielded so much power over everything that I did or was done to me in that environment. As I quickly came to understand, that's just the way it is in a psychiatric hospital. He had to write a pass for me to gain permission to do just about anything, including going home for a visit with my mother. Not that my mother really wanted me to visit her very often anyway. In fact, during the seven months or so that I remained a patient at Cedar Hills Hospital, I'm pretty sure that I only got to go home once. Oh, but that was a visit that I was not likely to forget.

When the day of my scheduled home visit dawned, I was feeling anxious about how it would all go. I knew that it was at least possible to enjoy time with my mother, but I didn't want my stepfather around and figured there was no way to avoid that. I was also not looking forward to being around my younger sister, mostly because within our family circle she was looked at as the good girl while I was the one who was always in trouble—the problem child.

As it turned out, I would have my mom pretty much to myself this time. When she picked me up in her blue Ford Mustang II with the white roof, she was dressed well, with fresh red lipstick on, and I was again struck by how beautiful she looked. She drove me to the home they still lived in on York Street, and pulled up next to the '47 Chevy pickup in the driveway. I wasn't so much excited to arrive at her house as I was relieved to get out of the car because as we were riding through my old neighborhood, I was terrified that somebody who knew me would see me and immediately go around telling everyone that "Crazy Kristy" was back.

It was about 10 in the morning, and as soon as we sat down, my mother cracked open a beer. Maybe it was her first one of the day, maybe not. I got a soda and she began telling me about all the problems in her life, but stopped after a couple of minutes and went to the mantel to fetch the big glass penny jar. Returning to the table, she distributed all the pennies evenly between us and announced that we were going to play penny poker. And that's exactly what we did, as she kept chugging beer after beer, for the next couple of hours. Finally, she got up and told me we were going out to the garage, half of which had been converted into a pool room. My father had taught me to play pool during his time with me, and the funny thing is that he taught me to play left-handed even though I was a righty, because he was left-handed and I still played that way. So my mother and I shot pool, as she continued to pound the beers. Beer, poker, pool—it was like a bar night out with my mother. This is how she chose to spend a rare block of time with her oldest daughter.

By this time, she was pretty drunk. Not wanting to be left out, but also steadfastly opposed to getting drunk again after what happened at that concert, I took a bathroom break and immediately started rustling through my mother's medicine cabinet. I knew she had her Valium in there somewhere, and sure enough I found it. After taking what seemed to be the right amount, I went back to the garage to shoot more pool. But my mom caught me, and we wrapped up our home visit with a big blow-up. I was still loaded when she took me back to Cedar Hills.

My mother scheduled one more visit with me weeks later, but that one didn't get very far. While we were still in the parking lot, she informed me that on this "home visit" she would be off doing something else by herself. I would be left to hang out for a few hours alone at the house with my sister. "Fuck that!" I screamed, and that was the end of that visit.

I spent that Christmas in my room at Cedar Hills. As the days crept by, I was feeling trapped, and terribly alone. How was I ever going to get out of the hospital? Even with the disengagement with my mother, I had moments when I would convince myself that things could still work out. Maybe there was something different I could do to make her want to have me home. Maybe if I could change, she would really open her arms to me. The only problem was that I had no idea what kind of change that could be. And that's when I'd just be swept up in a sense of total defeat. The only light shining around me were my moments playing volleyball and other games, because that's when I'd be around Richard. The longer I remained a patient at Cedar Hills, the closer I felt to him.

As much as I had been warned about what could happen, I was still taken by surprise when the news came one afternoon. A staff person named Craig, whom I hardly knew, called me into one of those small consultation rooms with two chairs and a little round table.

"You're being transferred," he said. "You're going to Oregon State Hospital. We had a staffing about you and the decision was made. You're leaving in two days."

"What...why? What do you mean? What did I do wrong?" I asked, and then the tears shut down my flow of questions. The move made no sense to me then. It was only months or years later that I figured out that the day Mr. Williamson was testing me with his rolled-up paper balls, I was already being penciled in to become a patient at Oregon State Hospital. It's just that at that time, the new children's unit of the state hospital had not yet opened, and since my parents had the health insurance to cover several months at a private hospital, the plan was to hold me temporarily at Cedar Hills. I never had a chance.

"You'll be okay," Craig said, reaching out to touch my back. By now, my sobs were subsiding.

"Where's Richard?" I cried. "I want to see Richard."

When he arrived a while later, he found me in the day room still trying to make sense of what was being done to me. They had warned me about getting sent off to Oregon State Hospital, but other than those few childish pranks, I had been good. Why did they still have to send me there now? I thought Richard looked sad, too, when he approached me and said he wanted to talk with me in a consultation room.

"I'm so sorry this is happening to you," he said after he closed the door and sat down by the table. "You know, I tried to get permission to take you as a foster child, but they said no because I'm a single man." He didn't need to add that him being an African-American probably had a lot more to do with it.

"I have something for you," Richard said, handing me a piece of white notebook paper with words carefully written in blue ink. The words were neatly arranged in short lines. Looking more closely, I could see that they were lyrics to a song: "Shining Star" by Earth, Wind and Fire. Richard had carefully copied every word, line by line. The message of the song is that no matter who you are, or what you may be going through, you are still a shining star and your life can take you somewhere you want to be.

I was crying too hard to say "thank you." Richard had just become one of my angels. And now we were having to say goodbye.

Soon after walking out of the consultation room, and watching Richard meander down the hall to prepare for his recreational duties, I went up to the nurses' station and asked for medication to calm me down.

"You don't have an order for anything like that," the nurse responded.

"Oh, well, that's okay," I said, trying to look far enough down the hallway to catch one last glimpse of Richard. *He wanted me to be his foster child*, I thought. I shuffled off to my room, just long enough to put Richard's song lyrics in a safe place, safe enough so that I still have them today, and then made my way back to the day room. When bedtime approached, I asked for permission to stay up later. I was afraid to be in my room, alone with my sadness. None of the staff objected. Most of them could be kind at times, and I know some of them liked me. But they had jobs to do, and their job never included showing me any real affection or supplying the kind of nurturing touch that children needed. It also never included being celebrated for anything special that I had done, or just for who I was. I was just one more mental patient to be monitored, evaluated and written about in the shift log.

When a night shift nurse sat down on the sofa beside my chair, she asked me if I had ever watched the TV show *Mary Hartman, Mary Hartman*. I told her I had never heard of it. We weren't allowed to watch TV much, and anyway I preferred to be in my room listening to the radio when I was free of school and other routines of the day and evening.

"Well, we all watch *Mary Hartman* every night," the nurse said, and invited me to watch. The program seemed weird to me, with this woman who was supposed to be an adult acting totally childish. I found out later that some episodes showed her having a nervous breakdown and being sent to a psychiatric hospital. Maybe that's why it was a big hit at Cedar Hills Hospital.

"I think it's time for you to go to bed now," the nurse announced after the TV show was over. I didn't argue, but I didn't sleep much that night or the next night, my last one before I was to become a patient at the state hospital. In the morning, as I walked down the hall for the last time, I was approached by Dr. Deeny.

"Hold on," he said, "I've got something I want to give you."

I allowed myself to look closely at my psychiatrist. He had really sparkly eyes.

"Something for your trip," he said, reaching into his pocket and pulling out two carefully wrapped gumballs. "I thought you might like to have something sweet." After I had taken the gumballs and thanked him, he said, "Oh, and one more thing." He had wrapped a bunch of quarters in Saran Wrap. "You might want a drink on the way, a soda or something," he added, and then he caught my eye as his gaze lingered. Yes, my doctor had always tried to do right by me.

Near the door that would lead me outside Cedar Hills Hospital, I was met by a familiar face. Cecily, my case worker, representative of the state that ruled over my life, held out her hand to greet me. In a moment, I would be climbing into the passenger seat of her gold Chevy Vega and heading off to another new home, another dark phase of life.

I hope she's got plenty of Merits, I thought. *Gumballs and soda can only take a girl so far.*

Cray Cray

6
The Real Cuckoo's Nest

***If you have ever seen the movie* One Flew Over the Cuckoo's Nest,** you got a pretty good look at the place that became my home on February 3, 1977. The movie that earned Academy awards for Jack Nicholson and Louise Fletcher was filmed right inside Oregon State Hospital, just over a year before my arrival. They tried to be realistic in portraying life inside a state hospital. The Oregon State Hospital director, Dr. Brooks, played an important supporting role in the movie and many patients appeared as extras or helped on the production crew. The main characters even slept on the adult ward for a while so they could better understand the experience of being a patient there. The movie portrayed the hospital as a dark, stark and creepy place ruled by the rigid hand of an inhumane staff.

I can't watch that movie. The cuckoo's nest captured in a Hollywood story is not just some fictitious place to me. It's real—much, much too real.

I have played hide-and-seek in the playgrounds of those mammoth grounds with the huge trees reined in by the 12-foot-high fences with the barbed tops so you cannot climb over them. I have ridden bikes in those dark, dusty underground tunnels that connect the many buildings of a facility that once held as many as 3,600 patients. I have witnessed Dr. Brooks, Randall McMurphy's doctor in the movie, doing his real hospital job. And I have watched or experienced many of the same kinds of behavior and treatment that shocked those who watched the movie, in a patient ward just a short walk from the filming location of the most striking *Cuckoo's Nest* scenes.

So, allow me to present to you now my real-life version of life inside the Cuckoo's Nest of the Oregon State Hospital…

As Cecily and I approach, the first thing I notice are all the locked doors you have to pass through just to get inside. After Cecily rings the buzzer box at the entrance, I can hear the turning of the key to unlock this first door. Soon after we step inside, Cecily is directed to an office on the right. In the hallway, I am told that I will need to have a physical exam. "I don't want any doctor in this place to look at me," I say to myself, and I bite my lip hard to keep from crying. I look down at the floor tiles and notice the distinctive pattern—two green, one white. I make the decision to try to step only on the green tiles. Not far down the hallway we come to a second locked door. The staff woman escorting me jingles a huge set of keys, unlocks this door, and closes it behind us with a clunk so loud it leaves an echo.

I see an elevator ahead and a door that appears to lead to the playground I had noted when we were driving up. As we walk on, we approach another door, the entry into Ward 40A of the newly opened Child and Adolescent Secure Treatment Program for children ages eight to eighteen. This third locked door is just as heavy as the first two. *Clunk.*

Entering the children's ward, I spot a boy crouched alone in an alcove rocking in place. We pass by the nurses' station separated from the rest of the ward by metal bars. Across from the station is a chair. "Sit there," I am told, and I immediately understand that they will be observing me. I wait, trying to look calm and relaxed. I feel dozens of eyes studying my every move. Carefully glancing around, I don't see any toys or games, which I was expecting now that I am on a real children's ward instead of being tossed in with adults and older adolescents at Cedar Hills Hospital.

Cray Cray

Not far down the hallway, I notice a ping-pong table. An adult male is playing against one of the boys of Ward 40A. When the man sees me watching, he puts his paddle down on the table and comes right over to my chair.

"You won't fool us," he says with a sly grin. I note from his badge that his name is Gerald. "You're trying to look like you're a nice girl, but we know the truth about you. We know how bad you are. We've got your number."

I feel the urge to raise my hand and show him just how bad I am, but I fight it off. I am determined not to give them any excuse for treating me worse than they're already planning to.

Before long, I am taken off my initial observation and brought to the girls' dormitory. I learn that there are 20 patients on the ward, but only seven girls. I am assigned a bed at the far end of the dorm, with a little locker for my stuff. I don't have much, mostly the clothes my mother picked out for me when I was first sent off to Christie School. When I am left alone to sit on my bed, I finally allow myself to cry. I am so absorbed in my sobbing, and counting the tiles on the floor, that I don't even notice that one of the other girls has come over to my bed. She hands me a box of tissues.

"Tears are good," Janie says, and then walks away. She is gone the next day, sent off to some other facility, I am told.

I soon get used to the rhythm of a typical day in the state hospital. We are awakened early in the morning by staff coming in and turning on the lights. We make our beds with military precision, part of what will earn points for our punch cards that measure our daily behavior. We get our cards punched for practically everything we do, from lining up on time for the next scheduled activity to washing our hands before eating. The big measuring stick is our "pinpoint," an individualized category for each person's primary goal to be focused on. For me, that's "expressing my feelings appropriately," which I guess means that when I get angry I don't wind up and smack the person who's pissing me off.

We walk in single file downstairs to the cafeteria for breakfast, which consists of Cream of Wheat, a slice of toast and disgusting looking powdered eggs that I mostly avoid. We eat in shifts, so we children don't mix with the adolescents. From the first day, I am assigned to the diet table. This upsets me. Yes, I did get a bit chunky from being on medication at Cedar Hills, but sitting at a diet table and being restricted to 1,000 calories a day? How can any kid survive on 1,000 calories a day?

After breakfast we line up, each person on her or his assigned square tile, and march back upstairs to clean up, brush our teeth and get ready for school. If we do all that according to the rules and in a timely manner, we get more points punched on our cards. School is held in a room downstairs beside the cafeteria. My favorite teacher is Bruce, because he's kinder and more cool than the woman teachers. I'm not concerned about catching up on all the school work I have missed because of my fifth-grade expulsion and getting bounced around three different places in the last year, but I do have one goal: to be named Super Student when the award is handed out every couple of weeks. Super Students get to go on special outings, and the first time I win it we go to a roller-skating rink where we all have a blast even though anyone there can see right away that we're the kids from the state hospital.

After lunch break, we go back to school until 2:30. Then we must sit on our beds for an hour or 90 minutes of quiet time, which is set up not so much to give us a rest from our busy day but to accommodate the shift change with its meetings and note-writing that makes it too hard for staff to keep watch over us. Late afternoon is the time for individual therapy or other appointments. Between those mandatory meetings we are free to float around and find something to do. There's only one toybox on the ward, an aquarium-sized plexiglass container with a few Teddy bears and toys. Down in the Rec area is a cabinet with a couple of games inside. The game that stands out to me is "One Bad Apple," with its cover description to "pick an apple from the barrel, but don't let the worm pop up." I seldom play but always fixate on the title: One Bad Apple. I imagine this is how Gerald and the other staff see me.

Sometimes someone is available to take us outside to the playground, where we can go on the swings or the Teeter-Totter, just like regular kids. I'm always up for joining in a game of kickball but shy away from softball because I don't like getting hit by the ball. My preference for these outdoor times, though, is just to sit by myself under one of the tall shady trees.

Dinner, like lunch, usually consists of some hard-to-distinguish meat, a ton of cabbage to keep us regular, and often the "soup du jour," a sloppy bowl of who knows what. The rumor that every patient hears in their first days in the hospital is that they use roadkill to beef up their soups. This rumor comes along with a known fact: in 1942, a week before Christmas, 47 people died and 467 got sick after eating dinner at the Oregon State Hospital. They all started vomiting or struggling to breathe after consuming that evening's scrambled eggs, laced with a poison used to kill the cockroaches that invaded the kitchen. Supposedly, the patient allowed to help in the kitchen that day made an honest mistake, reaching for the sodium fluoride instead of the powdered milk. Most of those who tell or hear the story don't believe that it was a mistake.

So we always have to be careful about what we eat, and how much, but this is where it pays to build up lots of points on your punch card. If you save up enough points, you can go to the canteen and redeem your points for soda and candy, which not only taste better but also are less likely to be poisoned than the roadkill soup and powdered eggs. Also, since the only dessert I am allowed on my diet is one graham cracker, I am desperate for anything sweet when I get to the canteen, where no one is counting our calories.

Once I get used to the daily routine, I begin to make a few friends. Michelle is a year older than me and very smart and sophisticated, Pam is okay except for intimidating me with her huge body, and Lonnie is easy to talk to. But my closest pals are two boys: Brian and Mark. Boys are not allowed on the girls' side of the dorm, but for some reason it is considered safe for us to go down to the boys' end. The big draw for me there is my friends' record player. We spend lots of time just sitting and listening together, no physical touching allowed, while rocking out to David Bowie, Peter Frampton and the Eagles' "Hotel California," which we love to sing along to when it comes to that part about being in a place where you can never leave. That's the way it feels to us kids as patients at Oregon State Hospital.

We don't watch much TV, except on Friday nights, but evenings sometimes mean an excursion to those scary underground connecting tunnels. That's where the swimming pool is located, and also where we occasionally get to ride bikes. I enjoy the activities down there, but you always want to move as quickly as possible in the tunnels because you never knew who or what might be waiting for you there.

On weekends, they don't serve hot breakfast in the cafeteria. Instead, we are handed small boxes of cold cereal and sit with our bowls and spoons on the floor of the hallway, arranged in a neat crisscross formation. As a real treat, Pam, the staff person in charge there, sometimes bakes us cinnamon rolls. One day she takes me into the little upstairs kitchenette and shows me how to make them. Saturday is cleaning day, which means assorted vacuuming, dusting and other chores, along with making sure our rooms are extra neat and tidy...

So that was the daily routine I followed as a patient in the children's ward of the Oregon State Hospital. It was a strange, tightly regimented environment, but I had to do my best to fit in. It was the only home I had.

Right from my transfer from Cedar Hills Hospital, though, I held onto one burning question: why am I here? Hadn't my behavior improved at Cedar Hills? Was I really so bad that I was going to be kept for months, maybe years, even forever, in a place that was more than 100 years old and that had once been known as the "Oregon Hospital for the Insane?" Was I still being punished for all those bad things I had done in the past? Or was I really ill?

Even as an adult, when I was able to obtain a copy of my hospital records, I have found no definitive and satisfying answer to those nagging questions. I discovered their list of my initial presenting problems:

Feeling avoidance, limit testing, stealing, assaultiveness, family conflicts, challenging authority, runaway risk, education.

Assaultiveness, was that even a word? Education was a mental problem? Just because I fell behind from being out of any regular school environment for a couple of years? And feeling avoidance—I didn't avoid my feelings, I just let them spill out in a rather demonstrative way sometimes. The other problems, I could understand. My official diagnosis, which I never heard until I saw the records as an adult, was "unsocialized aggressive reaction to childhood." In other words, I rebelled against being abandoned, neglected, belittled and mistreated as a kid. And that makes me crazy?

To add to the mystery, just six weeks after I entered the hospital my records indicate that most of those presenting problems, including my "assaultiveness" and being a runaway risk, had already been resolved. But I was still there, still regarded as a "mental patient." That was a growing part of my identity that I continued to fight against, but I usually seemed to be losing the battle. The staff, for the most part, reinforced my identity. At seemingly every turn, my behavior was pathologized. I was not allowed to sit at the same table as a new friend in the girls' dorm because I was "too dependent on her." Geez, isn't that what could be called a basic child need for friendship? And then I was judged for crying when a fellow patient was discharged from the ward, when it's totally natural to cry when you're in a strange environment and something familiar to you is taken away. And, of course, any time I got angry about the rules and how they were enforced, or anything else I didn't like, I was judged as being wrong, instead of being understood as a normal kid who gets angry and sometimes shows that anger in not so pretty ways.

I didn't need my own interactions with staff to be reminded of where I was. One day, Mark and I were allowed to ride our hospital bikes around the grounds. We headed right for the communications building, which housed the canteen downstairs. When a staff member buzzed us in, a woman patient was heading out. Being respectful of adults, we held the door open for her. She did not appreciate the gesture.

"You're following me!" she screamed. She was wearing mismatched clothes, oversized pants, her hair was wiry and disheveled, and the way her neck came out made her look like an ostrich. "You're tracking my thoughts, I know you are. But you're not going to get away with it. I know who you are, and I know how to take care of kids like you!"

We rushed inside to escape her tirade and immediately approached the staff person at the security counter to warn him about this wild woman on the loose. He just looked at us.

"Well, where do you think you are?" he asked, and then just stared at us a while longer until we went on our way. Right, we were in a mental hospital. In our own ward, we could observe the young boy who seemed to be constantly screaming and beating himself, and spent more time in restraints than out of them. Since the dorm room that I was eventually assigned to happened to be next door to the restraint room, I was reminded by the many screaming kids going in and out of there that I was among some true craziness.

Even when the staff tried to arrange "normal activities" for us, you never knew when you might witness some behavior that seemed to be, well, not so normal. The entire hospital got involved with planning "The Gong Show," an entertainment extravaganza to be held in the hospital's huge auditorium. Five of us girls from Ward 40A were going to perform the can-can. We were outfitted in the proper black dance leotard with the stretchy socks, and we practiced and practiced and practiced. Debbie, the recreational therapist, was helping to shape our performance, and Pam helped out as well. After a while, we were getting pretty darn good at our routine.

I was very excited when we stood off-stage waiting for our slot to perform in front of hundreds of patients, staff and administrators. I was going to be the first to lead us out there, as the live musicians played the song that almost everyone knows, and I was just hoping I wouldn't trip over myself as I got to the stage.

The act before ours was some kind of adult men's singing group, like a barbershop quartet. The four male patients were crooning like professionals until, in the middle of one song, one of the guys just stopped singing and walked right off stage. He just kept walking right past us, apparently responding to some kind of message in his brain.

Cray Cray

Immediately I figured that the other guys would be too confused or embarrassed by what happened to keep singing and hustle right off the stage themselves, so I took my first step forward.

"No, just wait, Kristy," Pam said. "Just let them finish. They'll be okay."

So, what was now the three-man quartet kept on crooning, and we waited for their act to conclude as scheduled before I led us out and we took over the stage. And we were great! When we completed our little dance, the audience showered us with loud applause. I was happy and proud, and although we didn't win any award from The Gong Show, Pam brought us all together back on the ward for a cinnamon roll celebration.

That was a great night, but another "normal" activity arranged by staff was not such a big hit for me. It all started when they introduced us to the Presidential Physical Fitness Award program. Staff had us down in the basement doing push-ups, sit-ups, pull-ups and all kinds of other exercises to whip us into shape and lift us toward the target fitness level. This was no cakewalk for a girl from the diet table, but I huffed and puffed my way through hours of stretching and straining, and when they gave the test, I managed to squeak by. *Whew, glad that's over with,* I thought. But no, this was just a warm-up for the real test: going on a couple of three-day backpacking trips in the woods.

As soon as they started talking about sleeping in tents, I felt a surge of dread. Camping didn't carry any fun memories for me, since I naturally associated it with my mother and stepfather's heavy drinking and arguing while my sister and I were quarantined in our little tent. And we'd be surviving on weird dehydrated food that would almost make us wish we were back in the Oregon State Hospital cafeteria. Eight of us would be going, mostly the older kids of the children's ward, and they had us prepare for the big adventure by putting on our backpacks and marching around in the tunnels. It felt like we were in the army.

Once we were ready to take on the outside world, they started us off small. We had a one-night warmup backpacking and camping trial run, which resulted in my coming back covered in cherry juice. At least I was allowed to take a long bath. But when we headed out for the longer trails and deeper woods, I simply had to deal with whatever we were expected to do. And on the uphill climbs on the switchback mountain trails, I wasn't dealing so well. Time and time again, I would fall behind the pack until one of the staff finally stopped the procession and walked back to attend to me and get me back onboard our little people train. When we finally put up our two-person, rust-colored tents, all I wanted to do was sit inside mine and not come out. I might have tried to run away, except I was too exhausted to even walk and had no idea where I was.

So, I survived the Cuckoo's Nest backpacking trip in that summer of '77. During that same period, I also was "awarded" the opportunity to go out in the hot sun and work at a blueberry-picking field. I was a bit more motivated this time when they told us it was a paying job, though I wasn't so excited about the schedule for the day. My friend Mark and I were awakened at 6:00 a.m., when the lights were still dimmed in the hallway. Pam had prepared our own individual servings of Cream of Wheat to start the day and packed us peanut butter and jelly sandwiches for our lunch break in the blueberry fields.

The next part seemed strange. Here we were, two kids living on a locked unit of a state hospital, with its grounds marked by high, protected fences, and we were going to ride un-escorted to the job site. They gave us two hospital bicycles and, since we had been there once with staff supervision, we were expected to find our way to the blueberry fields on our own. We rode and rode across the grounds, in the dim, early morning light, and then turned onto Center Street and bicycled through part of town on sidewalks. Fortunately, we did remember the way and arrived at the field on time to receive our little round buckets with the straps you put around your neck. As we listened to the supervisor explain how to properly pick blueberries, I noticed that we were among a crew of mostly adults. I couldn't be sure if they were state hospital patients or inmates from the nearby state penitentiary. Anyway, I did my best to follow the proper procedure, which was a bit like milking a cow in the way that you would bend the blueberry bush and coax the blueberries into falling into your bucket. By the time the hot sun had risen in the sky, I was getting pretty good at it.

Cray Cray

When our work shift was complete, with the steaming sun beating down on our bodies in the exposed blueberry field, it was already midafternoon. I was not only wilted from the heat but also still hungry since we had devoured our sandwiches by about 10 that morning. We got paid for our first day on the spot, and when Mark and I tucked our money away I came up with an idea.

"Let's go to McDonald's on the way home," I suggested, remembering how we had passed one on the way to work. "We won't get in trouble."

A few minutes later, I walked up to the McDonald's counter where I had enough money to buy a plain hamburger and a strawberry milkshake with change left over to take back to the hospital. As I savored this divine payoff for my hard work, I had another idea. The dining area had gotten pretty messy after the lunch crowd had breezed through, so maybe I could hustle up another job and make some more money that I could use to buy more McDonald's food. I got up and started picking up any trays or trash left on tables. I wiped the trays with napkins, deposited all the trash and tidied up the display area where people got their utensils and ketchup. Then I walked back up to the counter.

"I just cleaned up the dining area," I announced proudly. "It was a mess!"

"Well that was very sweet of you to do that," said the woman there. After pausing briefly, she added, "What kind of milkshake were you drinking?" A minute later I had my straw buried inside my second strawberry milkshake and gulped it all down in a flash.

"I'm going to get myself a real job here," I said to myself.

A couple of mornings later, when Mark was sick and had to stay behind at the hospital, I rode my bike off grounds with a new mission. Instead of biking all the way to the blueberry fields, I was heading straight for McDonald's. They hadn't even opened yet when I arrived because breakfast service had not yet become a part of every McDonald's location in those days. I sat by my bike and patiently waited, and soon after the doors opened in late morning and customers began giving their orders and making a mess in the dining room, I got to work. If anyone appeared finished, or almost finished eating, I would go right up to them and say, "May I take your tray for you? Here, let me clean off your table." Most of them smiled and welcomed the extra service, though a few looked at me a bit strangely. A worker at the counter even gave me a spray bottle and a rag so I wouldn't have to use napkins for my clean-up operations. With a joy I hadn't felt in months, I stuck with my task all through the lunch rush, certain that I would be rewarded with another free milkshake…or more.

Well, I did get my milkshake. But I also got a little talk from the manager.

"We appreciate you wanting to help us out," he said, "but I'm afraid you're not going to be able to do this anymore. You see, there are child labor laws that we have to follow. We can't have a girl your age working in our restaurant."

What? I can't work at McDonald's after all? But that was my plan! That was my ticket out of the Cuckoo's Nest.

The way I saw it, I had failed in my other attempts to run away because I didn't have the resources to take care of myself. But if I could get a real job, not just a week or two picking blueberries, then I could save enough money to go off on my own. Then I'd be free—no more lining up on the right-colored tiles, no more powdered eggs and soup du jour, no more punch cards, no more screaming kids fighting against restraints just outside my door.

With head hung low, I walked out of that McDonald's, hopped on my bike and pedaled as fast as I could. *It's not fair. I don't belong in the state hospital, and now I may never get out!* With my fury bubbling over, I didn't even notice the flower box sticking out into my path on the Center Street sidewalk. Wham! The collision flipped me off my bike, and when I landed I banged my knee hard. I was in so much pain, I could hardly pedal the bike. And when I limped back onto the ward, Mark pulled me aside and whispered, "You're in big trouble. They know you weren't at the blueberry field today."

I didn't know what kind of punishment they'd come up with, and I was fearing the worst when they called us all out for a group meeting right after shift change. So, what happened next was a total surprise. We were all lectured for some minor offense that I didn't even understand, and when a staff person approached me after the meeting all she said was, "Go take a long bath. Your knee will be fine." And that was that. My only real punishment for going to McDonald's and campaigning for a job instead of reporting for blueberry-picking duty was that I would have to keep living at the Oregon State Hospital. Which was more than punishment enough.

I need to point out that I experienced both good and bad in my treatment in the Cuckoo's Nest. And there was no question about the name of the person on the top of my "good" list. Gary was assigned as my primary therapist, and right from our first counseling session he won me over with his kindness. As a basic first question, he asked me why I believed I was in the state hospital. And as I cried and cried, he sat patiently waiting for me to speak.

"I don't know why I'm here," I said finally. "It's just that my parents, well, my mother and Jack, they don't want me. They don't know what to do with me. Nobody knows what to do with me or where I belong."

"I understand," he said softly. "Of course, it may be a bit more complicated than that, but I understand."

He didn't give me any lectures, didn't pull out a list of all the bad things I had done, didn't tell me I was there because I was crazy, didn't tell me he "had my number" like the other staff guy. Somehow, he really did seem to understand me.

Gary was a short man, although at five-six he was seven inches taller than me. He was Hawaiian, with short, pitch-black hair. He wore glasses, and he had a strong, fit body. I noticed that he always had his shirt tucked neatly into his jeans. Of course, I did have a crush on him, but not in any romantic way. I think all of us girls in that environment just naturally had some kind of crush on our primary therapist, someone with whom we would have a close and personal relationship, especially if the primary happened to be a cute guy a good bit younger than your father. But as the weeks and months of my stay at the Oregon State Hospital dragged on, Gary became something more important than the object of an innocent crush. In my fight to survive an upbringing of suffering and confusion, Gary would stand tall as one of my angels.

I will never forget the gifts he gave me on my 13th birthday. He told me ahead of time that he would be taking me out to dinner to celebrate, and he said that to properly prepare for the big night I should get some new clothes. From our arrival at the department store, I knew this was going to be a lot different from shopping with my mother before I left home for the first time. Gary made it clear that I was calling the shots. After careful deliberation, I chose a pair of baby blue corduroy pants and a navy-blue T-shirt with a red ribbed band around the edge. For good measure, I also picked out a Bohemian, blousy kind of shirt. I looked great, and I felt even better!

On the evening of April 27, 1977, I became a teenager in the Cuckoo's Nest. Gary and I passed through those three locked doors and headed out to a nearby Sizzler steakhouse. It didn't matter to me what I ate, only that I could eat a lot of it. I was off the diet table, with the calorie counter shut down, and I was thinking big things...like mounds of potatoes. I'm sure I had a piece of steak or some kind of meat, and some yummy fruit salad from the salad bar, but what I really remember is telling Gary how much I loved that huge, steaming hot baked potato slathered in butter and sour cream and hearing him say, "So let's order another potato for you, then." That was heaven!

Sometime during our meal, Gary began talking to me, but not in the way he would usually talk to me during our meetings in the little therapy conference rooms in the hospital. He explained how this was an important passage and invited me to consider what I wanted in my life. I responded that mostly I "just want out" and talked about not being wanted at home and about worrying that I was crazy and that I might be locked up for the rest of my life. Gary just listened, occasionally nodding.

"You know, Kristy, I don't think you belong in that hospital," he said. "I don't think you're crazy. You're very smart. And you want to know something else? You are going to do much more than this. Someday you are really going to do something special."

And there it was. This man Gary had just given me hope, a sense of possibility, when all I saw around me was hopelessness and despair. For a 13-year-old girl with a history of neglect and abandonment, mixed with blaming and labeling, I can't imagine a more precious birthday present. And I've never forgotten it.

And the night was not over. Rather than my usual graham cracker dessert, I was allowed to walk up to the soft-serve ice cream machine and build myself a whopping sundae, with whipped cream and candy sprinkles and whatever else I saw in front of me. After happily stuffing myself, we climbed into Gary's car for the ride back to the hospital.

"Would you like to see where I live?" Gary asked. "We can't go inside, of course, but we practically drive right by it. I can take a short detour to show it to you."

"Really? Wow, sure!" I gushed.

When Gary slowed the car down as we approached his house, I noticed that his garage door was open and a man was there fussing with a car. I could hear loud music thumping from speakers hung inside the garage. "That's my brother," Gary said. He honked but did not turn down the short driveway. I don't think his brother even heard us over the loud music.

"Do you like music?" Gary asked. When I said "sure," he cranked up his own car stereo system. I didn't recognize all the songs on his tapes because Gary appeared to prefer oldies, but I did know the words when Jimi Hendrix's "Purple Haze" came on. And all the way back to that place I didn't want to be in, we just sat silently together listening to the music.

It was past bedtime when I entered Ward 40A, but I had to tell somebody about my exciting birthday outing. Lonnie, my closest neighbor, was the natural target. She was a bit cranky at first when I tugged at her bed sheet, but then she caught on that I had a story to tell. We were always eager to hear stories about our primary therapists.

"I saw Gary's house," I blurted out.

"What? How?" she asked as she cleared the sleepy dust from her eyes.

I filled her in on the garage with the huge speakers, and *Purple Haze* on Gary's car stereo, and the two potatoes and the ice cream sundae at Sizzler.

"Wow, that is so amazing," Lonnie said.

"Yeah. Want to know the best part?" I said. "Nobody around us knew we were from the hospital. We were just like, you know, normal people."

That was another part of the gift. Gary had given me a sense of normalcy at a time and place when everything around me seemed crazy, and with his special message to me he also had provided me hope for the future. Yep, he was my angel. And I desperately needed an angel because as I continued to try to forge my way through the halls and tunnels of Oregon State Hospital, the real cuckoo's nest, I would come face to face with those from, well, the other end of the spectrum.

It began with the woman who assisted the girls at the shower. Her name was Ruth, and she worked the evening shift although not regularly. Showers were mandatory every night. The other female staff would just stand by close enough to be convinced we were really showering, but Ruth took the monitor role quite a bit further. She would stand right by the shower holding the little white perforated cups filled with shampoo and liquid soap, and when I was naked and under the water she would lean right in and pour that soap all over my body with her hands.

"I have to do this," she said, "because you have such poor hygiene." Well, I bathed every night. I knew that I did not have poor hygiene. I also knew that I would have to avoid Ruth at shower time at all costs. Of course, I understood that if I dared to say a word about this woman's totally inappropriate touching, no one would believe me and I would wind up being punished for making up stories about the staff. I was always the bad girl. "We've got your number," that staff guy had said on my first day.

I heard a different kind of message when I was "found" by another male staffer in the bushes during an evening game of hide-and-seek outside.

"You're becoming a young woman," Raymond said, "and I'm going to teach you about love." And then he reached into my pants and used his hands to show me what he insisted I needed to know.

I was confused. "Does this mean he's my boyfriend?" I asked myself, and again, I was convinced that I could never ask these kinds of questions to any of the adults on staff. I did find the courage to bring up what happened during hide-and-seek with a couple of the other kids, and it turned out that I was not the only one selected to receive these private lessons from Raymond. Hide-and-seek had taken on a whole new dimension for the young patients of Oregon State Hospital.

7
No Way Home

Looking back, I can see that it was never anything more than a young girl's fantasy. But in those first few months at Oregon State Hospital, it felt like a viable goal to focus on and pursue, a dream that I could still believe in. The dream looked something like this:

My family is going to decide they want me back home. My mother will finally see that I'm not crazy, that I'm not some dangerous animal, that I'm a good girl who just needs kindness, caring and unconditional love. She will finally divorce my mean stepfather, stop drinking and make a commitment to being a real mother to me and my sister. Someday she will come and rescue me from this horrible place and I will never go back.

During those dream moments, I still thought that if I acted "normal" enough in the hospital, and I didn't attack anyone or anything, the staff would tell my parents that I wasn't crazy and that of course they should take me back, and that they should seek out help for their own problems so they could act like real parents. I was convinced that I had that kind of power.

The evidence did not support my child's fantasy. Even before I was sent to Oregon State Hospital, the staff at Christie School had described a more realistic picture of my family:

Both the mother and stepfather have had enormous problems responding to Kristy in positive terms, and have succeeded in giving her the message that she is a hateful, out-of- control child who needs to be locked up. Their involvement in family meetings, campus visits, and other parent-child conferences at Christie School has been irregular and non-supportive... They view Kristy's problems to be independent of their own influence, resist most attempts to engage in family treatment... Kristy stands out as the "identified patient" in her family.

At Oregon State Hospital, my treatment team made at least an initial attempt to steer a family intervention. They invited my mother and Jack to a full meeting with me and staff, and when we were all together, they suggested that my mother and stepfather's role in helping me get better was just as critical as what the staff would be doing with me. Jack wasn't buying that argument, and neither was my mother. With their words and actions, they communicated their firm stand: "Kristy is the problem and you people in the hospital have to fix her."

When the next family meeting was scheduled, my mother and stepfather waited until the last minute and then called to cancel it. Jack was "sick." A day or two before the following scheduled meeting, they called the hospital with another excuse: the car broke down. And so it went. Occasionally they would agree for me to come home for a brief visit. One of those times at home was limited to two hours, a longer visit ended with Jack calling me all the old belittling names again and another scheduled get-together got called off at the last minute because my mother was too drunk. Instead of a commitment to open their arms to me, my family was putting up a wall of excuses.

The fantasies of a young girl do not die easily, however. I still held out hope for a miraculous change of heart, even as the hospital staff was helping me to accept at least pieces of reality. After one no-show at a family meeting, I told the staff that "If they were here right now, and I could say what I wanted to say to them, the roof would go sky high." Another time I had the insight that "I can't change to meet their needs" and that my mother was just not capable of loving me. When I got back to the hospital after one of those infrequent home visits, I reported that "my mom said I wasn't ready to come home to live, but

Cray Cray

I said she wasn't ready for me."

Still, I wasn't ready to hear the big news delivered to me at a full staff meeting. At least the person speaking the words I didn't want to hear was the one I liked and trusted the most.

"You're doing really well here," Gary began. "We think you'll be ready for discharge pretty soon. But Kristy, the truth is that you're never going to go home."

My fantasy bubble had finally burst. Gary gave me a moment to let those words sink in. I didn't blow up. I didn't turn and run out of the room. And I didn't cry. I just swallowed, hard, and kept swallowing and swallowing, as if trying to digest something that my insides could not handle. *Counting,* I thought. *I need to start counting something.* I began counting how many times I swallowed. *Four, five, six, seven...*

"This happens sometimes in families," Gary went on, resting his right hand between my shoulder blades. "But we are going to help you. You need a positive family and that's what we all want for you. We're going to find a place for you to live with another family, a family that will take care of you, a family that will love you."

He nodded toward Cecily, who also was attending the meeting.

"There are a couple of families looking at you right now," she added.

Cecily went on talking but I could no longer focus on her words. Reality had just smacked me on the side of my face, and everything I was hearing was just confusing me. Was I going to be adopted? Would I be sent to a foster home? What did it mean that some family was "looking" at me? Did they have my picture or something, and did they take it home and put it on their refrigerator so they could imagine whether they could accept me into their home, and into their lives?

Gary walked me out of the meeting room. He leaned down to close the gap between his height and mine, just as he had done when he took me out for my 13th birthday and at every meeting and conference with me. He wanted to show me that he was committed to looking at me not as professional-to-patient but as person-to-person.

"Why don't you just go rest for a while," he suggested in his soothing voice. "It's all going to be okay. We're going to figure this out with you."

I can't say for sure, but I imagine that if this had been anyone but Gary delivering this harsh blow to my soul and then trying to tell me to go chill, I probably would have lashed out in an expletive-filled, fist-flying outburst. But this was Gary. My angel.

I walked quietly back to my room and headed right for bed. Sitting cross-legged and staring at the wall, I began rubbing my fingers on the ribbed bedspread. Somehow that soothed me enough to keep it together. Fifteen minutes later, one of the staffers came in to check on me. It was Elwin, one of the nicer ones, though he didn't work many shifts on our ward.

"Just wanted to see if you were okay," he said. He asked me a few questions, but when it was clear that I wasn't going to respond, he added, "Wait here a minute. I'll be right back." When Elwin returned, he was carrying the guitar I had heard him play once or twice. He sat down on the floor next to the dresser, right in the line of sight where I was staring, and began to play. I didn't recognize the music, and he did not sing along. He also didn't try to talk to me anymore. He just kept strumming that guitar for five minutes, 10 minutes, 15 minutes—so long that I lost all track of time. Finally, he put down his guitar and looked up at me.

"Dinnertime," he said. "Can I walk you to dinner?"

He stood close by as I took my place in the line of patients waiting to have their hands checked, to verify that they had been washed. Elwin was in charge of the punch cards and when it was my turn, he remembered my pinpoint.

"So, did you express your feelings appropriately today, Kristy? What do you think?" he asked.

"I think I should get 20 extra points!" I said with as clear a voice as I had mustered since the start of the staff meeting.

"I think you do, too," he said, and he took my punch card and punched out even more than the 20 points I had suggested.

After dinner, we were told we could go down in the tunnels to the swimming pool. I decided to go along because I usually enjoyed swimming and thought it would be good to stay out of my room for a couple of hours. All through our swimming time, I was fine. But when we got out of the pool and dried off, the feelings began to rush over me. *Why didn't my family want me? Where is the staff going to send me? Is anyone ever going to really love me? What's going to happen to me?*

I didn't want to be around the other kids, laughing and joking and pretending that nothing was different about this night. I wanted to get back to my room, to rub my fingers in my bedspread and stare at the walls again. I wanted my own space.

I could not have been more than 10 paces ahead of the group when one of the attending staff called out.

"Kristy, come back!" he shouted. "You know you can't walk ahead of the group like that."

It was Gerald, the one who told me on the first day that he "had my number." I walked faster, trying to get away from his stern command and nasty look.

"Come back here right now!" he yelled in a louder, more forceful voice. When I still didn't turn around or even slow down, he ran at full speed to catch up with me.

"Just what do you think you're doing?" he shouted. He was trying to get his hands on both of my shoulders, as if to shake some sense into me. I never did like it when people who were angry with me for doing whatever I was doing tried to put their hands on me.

"Fuck you!" I shouted, my arms flailing. "I fucking hate you!"

Gerald ended up taking me down, right there in the tunnel, as I continued to curse until I lost steam and crumpled in a big ball of tears on the floor. And there he continued to restrain me, as the other staff person and all my fellow patients of Ward 40A walked past. He had humiliated me, made me appear like the bad person, the crazy girl, on the very day that I had been officially notified that my family was never going to love me and would never want me to live with them. That was the kind of treatment I had come to expect at Oregon State Hospital.

Maybe some of the other staff, like Gary, interpreted my tantrum in the tunnel for what it was, and maybe they even had Gerald's number and shook their heads in disgust at how he had responded to my behavior. Whatever the reason, not much was made of the incident, and I guess whoever was looking at me to see if they wanted me to join their family didn't get any pictures of me trying to beat the crap out of one of the professional caregivers of Oregon State Hospital. Because it wasn't long after that tunnel tantrum when I was called in for a meeting with our unit director.

"I've got good news," he said. "There is a couple who want to have a visit with you, to see if it would be a good idea to become your foster parents. They're going to have a visit with Lonnie, too."

Lonnie? I thought. *I didn't know Lonnie was due for a foster home. Does this mean we're in competition? Or is this couple considering taking both of us? What's the deal here?*

Since this wasn't Gary sitting across the table from me, I decided that I should keep my questions to myself. The first visit with Meryl and Tony was set up to be held in the hospital. When I met them, they told me they lived in McMinnville and that they had heard about me from one of the staff who worked mornings on our unit. That didn't interest me much, but when they told me they had one child, a daughter my age, my ears perked up.

"That's not good," I said to myself. "This girl lives with her family and they want her. She's not going to like me. I'll be the outsider. And they will never love me like they love their own daughter."

I kept my mouth shut, though, and the visit really wasn't so bad. When they came back a week later, I was given a pass to go out to a restaurant with them. This time, they brought the daughter, Helen, with them. I was surprised how friendly she acted toward me, and after we all had

Cray Cray

lunch and spent time at a park, Helen and I were crouched together in the bed of the little camper section that extended from their pickup. As we looked out the window together, and actually shared a laugh, my feelings about being scouted by this potential foster family were changing.

"I've got to get out of this hospital, and this is my shot, my ticket out. Maybe it's my only shot," I thought. "They're going to make a decision based on how friendly I act today. I better be nice to Helen. I've got to make this work!"

I remained on my best behavior, and I actually kind of liked Helen. I never did find out if Meryl and Tony also had a visit with Lonnie, but it didn't matter because they informed the staff that they wanted to take me home. I wasn't going to be officially discharged from Oregon State Hospital right away, though. Apparently, this was going to be like a trial run, and they were going to be able to decide whether to keep me or send me back after a few weeks or something. Sort of like taking a pet home from the animal shelter.

I guess the rules were that my foster parents could not come to take me from the hospital. I had to be driven to their home. Gary took me, and on the long ride we were much quieter than we would usually be together. I knew that Gary cared for me, and really wanted the best for me, and I wondered if he was more nervous than me about whether this was going to be the place that I would finally be able to call home.

It was getting near Christmas when I finally got settled in. I noticed right away that this family treated Christmas much differently than my family. Not that I could say for sure exactly how Christmas was going for my mother, stepfather and sister, because I didn't even get to go home for the holidays anymore. But I do remember from Christmases past that we would always have a real Christmas tree. This foster-tryout family had put up a store-bought, artificial tree. And their main staple for a seasonal treat were these strange pretzels with candy on them. That was a lot different from the food my mother would bring into our house by mid-December. We had all kinds of Christmas cookies, all heavily frosted, and dishes all over the house were kept filled with assorted candy. And there would be hot chocolate every day. Yep, my mother would go all out for Christmas.

Of course, I had to remind myself that her food celebration was driven by her eating disorder. And no matter how festive our home may have looked when decked out for the holiday, it didn't change the reality of alcoholism, bulimia, neglect and abuse. I guess I really didn't know what a true Christmas celebration in a loving home looked like.

Closing my eyes, I tried to imagine the actual Christmas scene with my ex-family in Aloha. During occupational therapy at the hospital, I had made little gifts for my mother, my sister and my stepfather. They were teaching us how to do ceramics and leather work. I made a keychain for my mother and some little zip pouch for my sister, but the project that really engaged me was my present for Jack. I made him a leather belt, giving careful attention to the buckle that I picked out and stamping his name on the back. I was giggling when I finished it, a response observed by the staff person supervising the project.

"So, who is this Jack?" Debbie asked, studying my belt.

"Oh, he's my stepfather," I explained, and I let out a full laugh.

"I see," she said and let me continue to enjoy my creation and the reaction that I anticipated him having when he saw it. Jack had given me the belt, so now I was going to give Jack the belt, too. It was pretty clever, actually.

Back in the home of my try-out family, they were making a big deal out of opening all their presents. In our house, we opened gifts in a free-for-all mode, with every person hunting down what was theirs and tearing apart the wrapping on their own. Not so with Meryl, Tony, Helen and all their relatives that had come to share the family Christmas. They all took turns opening their presents, and everyone watched the one person unveiling each gift. This concerned me. First of all, I didn't have anything for them. More important, they didn't know me and couldn't possibly have a good idea of what I might like. Sure enough, the main gift the adults had bought for me was a blue pantsuit that looked absolutely hideous. I thanked them politely anyway, and I was pleased enough with the bath products they had selected as my other presents.

Then it was Helen's turn. Her parents were not the only ones in the room that had picked out something for the girl who belonged in the family. She had a brigade of grandparents and aunts and uncles there, and each relative was determined to lavish more love on her than the next one. I watched Helen open up a bunch of art supplies, as well as material to do her own beading. When she unwrapped a fancy makeup palette, complete with eye shadow, I almost blurted out loud "I wish I got that!" but managed to stifle my response. Helen was far from finished. As I watched with mouth popped open, she added to her Christmas stash with all kinds of clothes, all totally beautiful and of course aligned with her favorite styles and brands. As she gushed and they beamed, I sat quietly, my hands folded on my lap. And I did some more thinking about this new living situation of mine.

She's their daughter, and I'm not. I might be their project, I might be their charity, I might be their mission, I might be a lot of things, but I am not their child. This is never going to work.

I began school right after Christmas vacation, joining the seventh-grade class in middle school. Right away, I discovered that my new schoolmates already knew of me as "the girl from the state hospital," thanks to my "sister" Helen. The taunting and bullying that had driven me to act out in my last round of public school just picked right up where it had left off. I was labeled, singled out as different. I was the crazy girl again. In school, I would never have the chance to just be a kid, to find some way to fit in, to do it right, to survive.

Fuck you, Helen. Fuck you, McMinnville. But you know what? I'm not going to stay. I'm going to get out of this mess.

I came up with an ingenious plan. I needed to make money if I wanted to run away and live on my own, and I already knew that kids bought and sold marijuana in a field on the way to school. Well, I had something more powerful than weed to offer. When I had left the Oregon State Hospital, I was put back on Thorazine. I didn't want to take it myself anyway so...

"I've got some really good stuff," I announced to a couple of kids when I took my place in the field while walking to school the next morning. "These are downers, and they will really get you loaded!"

"Really? Let's see," a girl a couple of years older replied. "How much?"

"Two dollars a pill," I said.

I made my first sale, and then another, and soon word got around about this hot new drug the girl from the hospital was selling. The eighth and ninth graders who had previously been satisfied with smoking pot were intrigued by the opportunity to try something new, something with a bigger bang for their buck. I sold at least 10 pills that morning before it was time for us to rush to school before first bell, and the demand had been established for a much bigger day to follow.

I was so caught up in the excitement of all those kids taking my Thorazine, I decided to take some myself, just to feel in sync with the crowd. Before lunch, in math class I believe, I began to sway. Soon I could hardly hold my head up. Yep, I got high on my own stuff, all right. I was loaded to the gills. I was so messed up, I began to panic about what was happening and found the nerve to get up from my seat in the back of class, stagger toward the front and tell the teacher, "I'm sick. I've got to go to the nurse's office."

"You're right. You don't look good," she said as she scrawled my name and her signature on a pass.

I looked inside the exam room and saw three other kids on or around the bed in there. They had their backs up against the wall and their feet sprawled out in front of them.

"Oh no," I said to myself. "Those are three of the kids I sold my Thorazine to. I've got to get out of here!"

While the nurse looked away to deal with the others, I moved past her office and headed to my locker in what seemed like slow motion. As I fiddled with the lock, trying to get my locker open and grab my stuff, I felt a strong male presence closing in on me.

Cray Cray

"You! You need to come with me right now," he said firmly. He was a cop. Ordinarily, I would try to run from his clutches, but I was not in any ordinary physical state. I allowed him to march me back down the hall, not to the nurse's room but to the administrative office. The office was already filled with other students, and I recognized every one of them from our little morning rendezvous in the field.

"Is there anyone else you gave that drug to?" he said loud enough for everyone in the office to hear.

"Well, I, uh, no, I don't think so," I said. "I think this is everyone."

"You better hope so," he hissed. "Just sit down and don't move. You've done enough damage for one day, young lady."

So I sat, alone, and waited. *What are they going to do with me now? Does this mean they're going to put me back in the hospital? If they do, will they even let me talk to Gary again, or will I get assigned to someone mean, someone who doesn't understand me? Or am I going to Donald E. Long again? I don't want to go to jail. I just need to get away from all of this, all these people. I want to be on my own. I can live on my own. I know what I have to do to make that work now. Maybe I can try another McDonald's or...*

"There's somebody here to see you," one of the principal's staff announced.

A couple of minutes later, I had settled into a familiar spot, sitting cross-legged in the passenger seat of a gold-colored Chevy Vega.

"Quite a morning, huh?" Cecily said, handing me a cigarette.

"I just needed some money," I said.

"I see," she said with a nod.

"Where are you going to take me?" I asked.

"Well, you're not going back to Meryl and Tony's house. Your placement there has been...they're done. So, tell me, Kristy, what do YOU want to do now?"

"I want to go home," I said, because I knew I couldn't just say I wanted to run away to Portland, get a job, live on my own, and never have to deal with any of this again. "To my mother."

"Oh, you know that's not going to happen," Cecily responded. "Here's what I think we're going to have to do now: I'm going to take you to an emergency shelter for foster children whose placements didn't work out."

I could hear the disappointment in Cecily's voice, and I flashed to how Gary was going to receive the news. He really wanted this foster home to work out for me. He wished that I could be with a family that would love me, some home where I could get a fresh start. He had told me that I was going to do something more someday. But how?

"I don't know how long you will be there," Cecily added, "and I'm not sure what will happen next. Just do your best, Kristy. And try to stay out of trouble."

Trouble? Me? Why would she think I might get in any trouble???

8
He Was Going to Teach Me What Real Love Is

Cecily pulled to a stop in the driveway of a small house in the middle of nowhere. This was the emergency shelter she had told me about. She took me inside and introduced me to an elderly couple by the name of Fletcher or Farmer or something. They showed me two bedrooms, one for boys and one for girls, each with a bunk bed. One boy was already staying in the boys' room, and I was going to have the girls' room to myself for now.

The whole house was dark, smelly and cold. The only heat came from a fireplace that didn't send much warmth to the bedrooms. The couple just sat in their living room chairs, right up close to the fire, and watched TV. I was informed that the eating routine would be cold cereal for breakfast, lunch at school and then a warmed up frozen TV dinner at night. I found the old folks scary and decided I would stay out of their hair as much as possible.

The good news was that I was going to be in a new school where the kids didn't yet know me and my reputation. The bad news is that on the first day of school, I got sick. This time, I had not taken any drugs. I was just sick. After watching me vomit a couple of times, the school nurse called my "home" and told the shelter couple to come get me.

They never did. I wondered if they could even drive. When I came home from school and didn't even eat my TV dinner, or my cold cereal the next morning, they sent me back to school anyway. That's when I knew that it was time for me to take matters into my own hands.

The emergency shelter was in Forest Grove, an hour or so from Portland. I couldn't afford the bus fare, so I would have to hitchhike. I didn't mind. I was used to thumbing rides. It was still morning when I got to the city, and from past experience I knew just where I wanted to go. After a long walk, I entered Arbuckle Flat and hustled to the meditation room to catch up on my sleep. The coffee shop and hippie hangout where I had once hidden after running away from Christie School was still going strong. They still played acoustic music at night, and they had some kind of bulletin board with information for runaways. I didn't need to read whatever they posted up there. I was a girl used to figuring things out on her own. The important thing here was that the people around Arbuckle Flat, who had to have known that I was one of those runaways, basically left me alone.

After a couple of days, I made friends with another girl. She was maybe a couple of years older than me, and she told me she actually had a place to stay.

"Can I stay with you a couple of days?" I asked her.

"Uh, yeah, I guess so," she said.

When the police caught me, I wasn't sure whether my new "friend" had anything to do with it or not. All I knew was that I was in trouble—again. After I was processed at the Donald E. Long Detention Center, Cecily showed up to retrieve me. She told me that this time I was being assigned to a group home and that they had a bunch of girls already living there. I was sure to be able to find some friends and a way to fit in.

At least the place wasn't dark and smelly, and the couple running things were not so old. They lived on the main level of the house, and I was going to be one of eight girls living down in the basement. They had staff helpers who would come in and oversee us sometimes, but we were free to spend a lot of time on our own. I was the youngest girl, but going back to my hospital days I was used to that. It was easy to find my place in the group, especially when we would hang out together outside at the picnic table smoking cigarettes. Smoking, as I had learned, was a real bonding activity for teenage girls like us.

Our group included twin sisters, Donna and Debbie. I thought they were beautiful, and very sure of themselves, and I devoted extra effort to getting close to them. *If I can be friends with them, this place won't be so bad,* I thought. *It's not like that foster home with the daughter where they were trying to squeeze me into that fake family thing. This is more...real.*

So things were going okay in this new home for a while because I had friends with me. I even tried to make some friends at my new school. Academically I was still lost, unable to catch up at what was probably my fourth school in seventh grade. Socially, though, I thought I had a chance. The other kids knew that I was living in a group home, but somehow that wasn't as much of a stigma as just getting out of the hospital or staying in some emergency shelter. I tried to reach out, and this time something different happened. Instead of being rejected, I was doing the rejecting. Once I got to talking with some of these other kids, I found their lives to be dull and mundane. The town we happened to be going to school in was named Boring, and the name fit these girls perfectly. "I live a *much* more interesting life," I said to myself.

And what was that interesting life? A merry-go-round of fighting and running, moving from one bed to another, or sometimes no bed at all, being escorted all around the Portland area by some woman who worked in Children's Services and who let me smoke cigarettes in her car, being told I was not wanted, that I was crazy. Sure, I led a very interesting life...

Looking back, I can see that I didn't click with "normal" girls because I had assumed the strong identity of a girl who always got in trouble. That's how I had come to define myself, and that's the box I found myself wedged inside. I was a troublemaker, a real bad-ass. You didn't want to mess with me.

Donna and Debbie, being older teens, had been living interesting lives even longer than me. Figuring that I could learn a lot from them, I began to shadow them around. They would leave our group home often, sometimes legitimately with passes given out by the couple upstairs and other times just sneaking off on their own. Naturally, I wanted to go with them. I was always ready for some new adventure.

"No, Kristy, you can't come with us," they would say. "You're too young for where we're going."

Me? The girl with a history of running away to Portland and finding ways to survive for days at a time? The girl who knew her way around psychiatric hospitals and kids' jails and who had once stormed out of a courtroom after screaming "Fuck you!" at the judge and then ripped a phone halfway off the wall? Me, too young?

It wasn't long before I had convinced the twins to take me along on their next outing. I think the three of us had finagled passes, and instead of having to hitch a ride from our little town of Boring, somebody actually picked us up and drove us into Portland. We got dropped off at a rather large house, and as soon as I stepped inside I could see that a party was going on. These weren't kids messing around with a few joints. These were tough young men having a real party.

I was scared. The truth was that although I could handle drugs, I had never touched alcohol after that one time at the concert with Richard from Cedar Hills Hospital when I downed two glasses of wine and got sick. Anyway, the smell of beer always reminded me of my mother's drinking, and her drinking problem was part of the reason that she couldn't be my mother.

I noticed right away that two of these beer-chugging guys were apparently the boyfriends of Donna and Debbie. When they scooted off with their guys, I found a spot on the sofa and sat motionless, almost paralyzed.

"Hi there, I'm Percy," one of the guys said as he approached me. He looked like he was at least 25 years old. "You're not drinking anything. We've got to do something about that. Come with me."

Something about his voice told me that I should follow him, and when he took me into the kitchen, opened the refrigerator stocked with alcohol and handed me a Schlitz Malt Liquor, I accepted it. He got one for himself too, and he handed me a Dixie cup to pour mine into. That seemed like a kind thing for him to do.

I sat at a dining table and started drinking with Percy, and soon a bunch of the other guys crowded around us. It didn't take long for me to start feeling woozy.

"Hey, let me have your arm for a minute," one of the guys said to me and, without thinking, I held out both arms. He rolled up the sleeve on my left arm, picked up some kind of marker, and wrote some numbers on my skin. A phone number. Then another guy came in and wrote his number on me, and then another and then another. In my woozy state, I didn't find this scary. In fact, I started laughing. "Why are they writing their phone numbers on my arm?" I said to myself.

Then the wooziness was accompanied by stomach upset. "I think I'm sick," I told Percy. "I need to lie down." He smiled. "Sure, sure," he said, and he escorted me up a narrow stairway into what appeared to be a converted attic. It was a tight space and as I looked around, all I saw were beds, a whole bunch of single beds scrunched in close. The low-level ceiling was draped with a real parachute that someone had tacked up there. The room was pretty dim and I couldn't make out everything else, but as we walked past one of the beds I began to hear noises. Glancing toward the bed, I could see enough to realize that the female with one of the guys I had seen upstairs was Debbie. I knew enough to understand what they were doing, and my only thought was that I should be careful not to interrupt them. We walked past another bed with two other people making sex noises until finding an unoccupied bed.

Percy motioned for me to lay down and sat on the edge of the bed. He smiled again, and then he leaned down and kissed me. What's happening? I thought he knew I was sick and just needed to lay down and rest and...When he began to get forceful, I tried to call out "Debbie! Debbie!" but my words were coming out muffled, and then he put his hand over my mouth just to make sure and he got more forceful and

I tried to squeeze my body out from under him and it hurt and then I just got frozen. "I'm going to teach you all about making love," he mumbled in his beer breath that I could smell more intensely because he was so…close. "That's right, little girl, I'm going to teach you what real love is." **Be still, be still, he'll be done soon.** When he finally got up, he saw the blood on his penis. "Dirty bitch!" he growled. "Go clean yourself up." Before I could move, I noticed that part of the parachute had come off the wall and was tangled up in the bed sheet. It had blood all over it.

I didn't cry. I just felt confused. Was that making love? Was Percy really going to teach me what real love is?

"Well, hi there," a female voice said. "I guess you weren't too young to come with us to our little party. Come on, let's get you dressed."

Debbie seemed so matter-of-fact about what happened. Didn't she know I was trying to call out to her to get him to stop? Maybe she knew this was going to happen. Maybe this was something she believed I needed to be taught. I was still confused.

When I got downstairs, all the guys were laughing at me. At least, that's how it seemed. Percy was with them. He told me to take my arm out and, in bigger writing than the other guys, he wrote his number on my skin. "Call me," he said firmly.

Getting back to the group home is just a blur to me now. I do remember that there was a staff person in the basement when we got there, but she didn't talk to me. She did speak to Donna and Debbie, though. I didn't sleep that night, and the next morning Donna came to me and told me I had a phone call. There was a phone on the wall with a little high stool to sit and talk at in our living quarters, but this was the first time anybody had called me.

"Hello, love," the male voice on the other end said when I picked up. "I just wanted to remind you that any time you want to come back to me, just let me know. Remember, I can teach you what real love is."

"Uh, okay," I mumbled, and then I hung up.

Cray Cray

Fortunately, our night in the attic with the scrunched-together beds and the parachute on the ceiling had taken place on a Friday night, so I had the weekend to stay inside. On Sunday, the house mother came downstairs and told me to come up to her office. *Oh no, she knows I've been drinking. I'm going to be in big trouble again.*

"I know what happened," she said. "You had sex. What we do with our girls who have had sex is get them on birth control. We're setting up an appointment for you early next week."

I stayed in the group home long enough to go to my doctor's appointment, where nobody asked me any questions about how I came to have sex. They just gave me my birth control. By the following weekend, I was gone.

The first thing I did when I got to Portland was to call Percy. "Maybe he really does love me," I said to myself. I was a girl, just on the brink of turning 14, who was so desperate for love. And when we got together, he knew just the right words to make me believe it.

"Nobody else wants you, but I want you," he said. "Stay with me. This is where you belong."

So I stayed with him in the northeast Portland house he was living in. His mother was living there with him, but Percy made it clear from the outset that I would not be sleeping in the main part of the house with them. He told me that I would be staying downstairs, in the unfinished basement. It did have a TV, a beat-up old sofa and a bed with springs hanging out. Mostly, I sat there alone and watched TV. Percy would come down and bring me food, and he would talk to me, always reminding me how he was teaching me about love. After we had sex, he would go back upstairs to sleep. I didn't mind. I believed he was my boyfriend but that I had to stay downstairs for the night because I was so young...or something.

I never met his mother, although at times I would hear her talking loudly about me: "Is she still down there? When is she going to leave?" I couldn't hear what Percy said in response to her, but it always seemed to end the argument. He was the one in control.

"You really love me, don't you?" he asked me one evening. When I half-nodded, he went on. "Yes you do. In fact, you love me so much you would ho for me, wouldn't you? One day I'm going to take you over to Killingsworth Avenue."

I did understand what a "ho" was. I even recognized that this was probably what Donna and Debbie had been doing in Portland all those times they snuck out before taking me with them. And, yes, I really did believe that he loved me and that I loved him…loved him enough to do anything for him.

A week later, Percy took me to the area around 4th and Clay, a known Portland prostitution strip. Coming to a stop, he pointed to a girl and told me I should go and talk with her and she would explain exactly what I needed to do.

"I'll be right nearby," he said. "Then afterwards we'll go have dinner."

The girl appeared to be about 18, maybe 19.

"Honey, just come with me. I'll show you how this goes," she said. "You just stand right over there and you wait for a car to pull up. Then you walk up to the window and you ask him 'Do you want a date?' That's all you have to say. Then you set the price."

When she explained the prices for the different categories of services, I tried to act as if this was a totally natural and common work assignment. I listened closely to her instructions. I wanted to do this right.

The first patron drove me behind a building, and when he was done he drove me back to the pickup spot. Percy was waiting for me.

"I'm real proud of you, girl!" he beamed, as he held out his hand for the money that I had been paid. "Now let's go spend some of that money. We're going to have ourselves a real good time."

He took me to a Burgerville, Portland's own hamburger chain. It felt like I was on a date. Yes, my boyfriend loved me so much that he was taking me out on a real date.

So that was my job for much of the summer of 1978. I got better at

Cray Cray

asking the right questions, and I would stay out for longer shifts. Percy didn't take me out to dinner all the time, or actually very much at all after a while, but I didn't care. He loved me, and he was taking care of me.

I don't know how long this relationship would have lasted if the police had not picked me up. I'm not sure what I had done wrong to get caught that day, but when they plucked me off the street I knew they would not be taking me back to my boyfriend's house. The state of Oregon was still in charge of me, and this time they had me delivered to some kind of group foster home that just happened to be right down the road from my mother and stepfather's home in Aloha. The place even reminded me of that house: dirty, unkept, kind of icky.

There were three other girls staying there, and once again we were assigned to live in the basement. Wendy and Bruce, the house parents, had three daughters of their own, but it was made very clear that we would not be mixing with them. We would only come upstairs to take a shower, do our assigned cleaning chores or get a plate of food, which was to be brought back downstairs immediately. We had our place and were expected to stay in it. Instead of joining a family, we were outsiders living under an arrangement. This time, we didn't even have a staff person coming around to check up on us.

It didn't take me more than three or four days before I started sneaking out at night. Naturally, I called Percy right away. When I would ask him if I could come see him, sometimes he said yes, and I would stay long enough to get back on the street for an hour or two. Sometimes he would spend time with me afterward, sometimes not, but he did not invite me to stay in his basement again and I would soon make my way back to my group foster home. Other times when I'd sneak out and call him he would say, "This isn't a good time."

Slowly, reality began to seep into my thoughts. *Maybe he's not really my boyfriend, after all. Maybe he doesn't really love me, and he's just been lying to me all this time. Anyway, why should he want me? Nobody wants me.*

Soon even darker feelings were washing over me.

If I can't stay with him, I have nowhere to go, no place where anybody will love me and take care of me. I have no future. My whole life is hopeless.

Those thoughts kept spiraling and spiraling in my brain, and I knew I had to do something to make them stop. The next time I got out by myself, I rushed to the pharmacy and grabbed the first over-the-counter medication that looked like it could work. I took all the pills down with no hesitation and waited…

"You'll be fine," said Elena, the older girl in the home and the only one that I talked to much. I had thrown up, big-time. My overdose had not gone the way I expected. Elena did not say one word to Wendy and Bruce.

I still felt miserable, but my despair slowly shifted toward a sense of determination. "I have to give this thing with Percy one more try," I said to myself. "Maybe if I tell him that I am not leaving Portland, that I won't be going back to any group home, that I will commit to being what he wants me to be, maybe he'll change. Maybe he'll love me again. I have to try."

I gathered the few belongings I had and hitchhiked to the city. As soon as I got there, I headed straight for that house I had lived in with Percy. I didn't even call. I figured if I just showed up, if I surprised him, he could see how much I loved him, how much I wanted him, and he would take me back. The only problem was, the house was vacant. There was no sign of Percy, or his mother. *Now what do I do? I can't go back to that foster home. They won't let me back. I'm here, I've got to figure out how to survive.*

Needing money to buy time to figure out what to do next, I went to 4th and Clay and turned a few tricks. Then I thought of Donna. I had run into her one day soon after I began this work, and I had a number for her. When I called her, she told me where we could meet, and as soon as I saw her I asked if she knew anything about Percy. Where was he? Was he still in Portland? How could I find him?

"Oh, him," she said with a frown. "He's in jail. They busted him."

"Arrested?" I said. "For what?" She looked me straight in the eye.

"For rape," she said.

"Oh my God!" I gasped. "He raped somebody? That's terrible. Are you sure?"

I sort of understood what rape was, but not enough to make any connection to my first experience with Percy. I just didn't see him as a person capable of doing something so horrible. My comprehension was still stuck somewhere in that vast terrain between early adolescence and adulthood. *But he was my last hope, somebody who was going to love me!*

"Kristy, he's gone," Donna said. "But let me think if there's some way I can help you."

A few hours later, she had hooked me up with a prostitute friend who happened to be a single mom with two kids. She had been looking for someone to take care of her children while she was out working, but she had limited resources to offer. Our deal was that in return for watching her kids, she would provide me with food and shelter. The kids weren't so bad but the house had no heat. I made it through most of autumn, but once the chill of December settled in, I got the urge for going. Of course, if I was going to give up this free roof over my head, I was going to have to make some money to afford a warm room to sleep in. I had been feeling tired and achy, with a constant runny nose, for at least a week, and in the last few days a deep cough had come on. But there was no way I could see a doctor because, even if I could afford it, I'd be caught right away. I just had to keep on going, and doing what I needed to do.

By now, it was only a few days before Christmas. Tis the season to be whoring, I thought flippantly. This time I staked out sidewalk territory in another hot spot near one of the Portland hospitals. With most working men getting extra time off for the holidays, business was good. All was going well enough until I got picked up by a guy in a van who decided not to follow the rules of the trade. As soon as he stopped the van and pulled me in close, he ripped open my shirt. That was just the first signal of how he intended to spend our arranged time together. His rough treatment was more forceful than Percy had been with me that first time, and I had no one looking out for me now. Fortunately, the asshole, ignoring my cough, achieved the results he wanted quickly and was soon opening the door of the van for me to get out.

I tried to slow my staggered breath, but I did not cry. Bad-ass girls do not cry, I reminded myself. I pulled my coat over my torn-apart shirt. By now it was getting cold, very cold. Looking up and down the street for signs of danger, I had a sudden realization: it was Christmas Eve. I stumbled to a pay phone and called the only number I could think of trying in a state like this.

"Can I come home, just for Christmas?" I blurted out as soon as my mother picked up the phone.

"No, you know the state would not let you do that," she said. "You can't come home. That's just the way it is…but Kristy, I have a present for you."

"You what? What kind of present?"

"It's a blow dryer."

I slammed the phone down so hard it bounced right off the receiver and dangled by its cord. I kicked the door to the pay phone open and stepped back into the cold night air. *A blow dryer? What the fuck am I going to do with a blow dryer?*

After circling the block, I went back inside the pay phone. Straightening the tangled cord and placing the phone back on the receiver, I finally got a dial tone. I had one more call I could make: Kathy. She was a friend, but a different kind of friend than Donna and Debbie. She didn't live in any group home or in foster care; she actually had her own family and a real home. I had met her at school when I was living in that basement of my group foster home, and because she had just moved into the area, she didn't know anything about my reputation. Her family was from New Mexico and they looked different than the kids from Oregon. For some reason, I just felt like I could talk to her. I told her about my background, on my terms rather than the way the kids at school would spin it, and she didn't care. Even though we were so different that she didn't even smoke cigarettes, she just accepted me for who I was. I didn't have to reinvent myself for her.

It was also about this time that I stopped referring to myself by the name Kristy as part of my effort to leave my childhood behind. I decided that I'd be Kris from now on, and that's what people would call me. Soon after we first met, Kathy had begun inviting me to come over to her house after school, and since she lived only a few blocks from my little shared basement, it was easy to hang out for hours at a time and then slip back into my place late in the evening. What a house! It was strewn with books and toys, and filled with life. Kathy's mom was bubbly and chatty and friendly to me. I felt like I had just walked into the home of *The Brady Bunch*. Hanging out with Kathy was always fun and a nice break from the other company I had been keeping and the places I spent most of my time.

Now, on Christmas Eve, I really needed another one of those nice breaks.

"Can I come see you?" I asked Kathy on the phone. "I need a shower and some clothes because my shirt got ripped off when I was...and it's cold as shit out here, Kathy. Can I just come up there for a little while?"

"Well, yeah, I guess," she said. "I mean, I want to help you. But Kris, where are you?"

"Oh, well, I'm in Portland now but I can get a ride out there, no problem. I'm good at that."

"Kris, be careful!"

I didn't try to hitchhike out of the city that night. I got a few hours' sleep on the sofa of one of the other street workers I knew. She had a small fake Christmas tree in the corner of her living room with two wrapped presents under it. Bright and early in the morning, I was on the road. Traffic was light, but catching rides was easier than usual.

"So where are you going?" I asked a couple that had stopped to pick me up. They didn't look at me suspiciously, though they did seem confused.

"Oh, you know, just going home for Christmas," I said and tried to fake a smile.

A few hours later, I reached Kathy's house. As I turned into her driveway, I suddenly felt uneasy about how my arrival would go over with her family. I wasn't used to dealing with "real" families. I decided that I should duck down under one of the living room windows and scope out the scene. Peeking my head up, I felt like I was looking into a Christmas card scene. Everyone was laughing, hopping around, acting silly, hugging one another. It wasn't like my foster home with Helen and the spotlight on each person unwrapping every single present. This was...real.

For the first time since I decided that I had to get out of Portland, a few tears welled up. Sometimes you really don't know what you don't have until you see it right in front of your face. *I can't knock on their door right now. They're having Christmas. Anyway, if I show up there right now they'll know I'm living as a runaway.*

So, gripping my coat tighter around my body, I trudged the few blocks back to the group foster home. I could not return there anymore because I had run off. If the house parents found me, they would call my caseworker and they'd just send me back to Donald E. Long or another one of those awful shelters. I had burned my bridges.

Still, I needed someplace to get warm and rest. When I staked out the group home, it was clear that the house parents were out. I snuck into the empty basement, but I barely had time to take off the chill when I heard noises upstairs. Thinking quickly, I lifted up a sheet that was covering stacks and stacks of newspapers, climbed on top and pulled the sheet over me. I was still there, breathing silently and trying hard not to cough too loud, when Elena came in.

"Elena, Elena, it's me," I said softly, still concealed in my perch.

She jumped. "What? Kris! What are you doing here? I thought you left. Everybody thinks you ran away."

"Yeah, I know," I said, lifting off the sheet. "It's okay. I'm back in Portland. But, you know, I just had to get away for a while. I'm hungry and I need a shower. I was going to go over to Kathy's because they don't know I'm a runaway. But, well, it's Christmas. I just want to crash here tonight and then I'll go."

"Okay," she said. "But you can't go upstairs to take a shower. They'll catch you."

"You're right," I said. Rummaging around the basement, I found a few clothes I had left behind and managed to change into something that was not torn or filthy. I sank down into my old bed, still keeping an ear out for any signs of the house parents coming downstairs. "Merry Christmas," I mumbled to myself.

When I woke up early and looked outside, I noticed that it was raining, or maybe it was sleeting. I ran most of the way to Kathy's house, but I was still soaked and freezing. I rang the doorbell, clutching my tote bag with the few clothes I had plucked out of the basement the night before.

"You made it!" Kathy gushed as she opened the door. After saying a quick hello to her mom, who had already cleaned up from Christmas, Kathy and I rushed to her room. Kathy wanted to know everything that had happened to me since I ran away, but I was careful with what I chose to share, leaving out the details about going looking for my boyfriend who was sort of a pimp and finding out that he was in jail because he had raped somebody and then having to make a few dollars and getting picked up by a guy who didn't play by the rules…I left out all of that. I mostly told her about how I had hitched up from Portland and snuck into my old group home and hidden on top of the newspapers with a sheet pulled over me. That was enough.

After lingering a few extra minutes in the best shower of my life, I let Kathy curl my long hair. We just hung out doing our makeup together, doing girlie adolescent things. When she told me all about her Christmas, I did not let on that I had peered in through the window. Kathy's mom made us lunch and the afternoon drifted by lazily and peacefully. I was asked to stay for dinner, and sitting around the table I still felt as if I really had walked into the home of the Brady Bunch. Settling back into Kathy's room, I tried not to think about what I was going to do, or where I was going to go next. It was after 10 p.m. when her mom came in.

"Okay girls, I think it's time to say goodnight for now," she said in a kind tone.

"Oh, yeah, I should go," I said, trying to think of where I would actually go to. Maybe I could get one more night in the basement with Elena, and then I could go back to Portland, maybe find one of the other girls who needed a helper in her home. Maybe, maybe, maybe.

"I know what we'll do," Kathy said as she walked me to the front door. "After you get outside and my mother can't see you, I'll push some blankets out my window. You can sleep in my sister's car tonight. It's the Nova right over there."

Kathy executed her end of the plan fine, and I climbed into the back of her sister's car. The sleet had turned the sidewalks and the street icy. It was getting colder and colder. As I tried to get comfortable inside, I noticed that a good chunk of the rear window was cracked, and between some of the cracks were a few good-sized holes. This was not going to be a warm, cozy sleeping spot.

Wrapping myself in the two blankets Kathy had tossed me, I was already shivering and my cough was getting deeper and more persistent. I looked for something to count, to try to calm down, but I couldn't find anything. I just tried to burrow deeper under the blankets, but after a bit they were frigid, too. Realizing that sleep would be impossible, except maybe for a quick nod-off once in a while, I just tried to lay still. You can do this, you can do this, you can do this. Only seven more hours and I could get out and get moving again. Figure out a plan. "I'll be okay," I said to myself.

Maybe.

9

In the Womb, Part I

The sleet had mixed with snow during the night. Lying awake, I could make out the sound of a newspaper skidding across the surface of the driveway after the delivery man tossed it. Then, sometime later, I heard another sound. *Crunch, crunch, crunch.* Someone was walking down the driveway, apparently heading out to pick up the paper. I crouched lower on the back seat, which was frigid to the touch. Everything in the car was practically frozen. And the crunch, crunch was beginning to get closer to the Nova...and me. "No, no, they can't find me here," I said to myself. I tried to hold my breath but couldn't contain a few muffled coughs.

Then I saw her face, the coral lipstick—she was coming right up to the rear window on the driver's side of the car. She opened the front door and, with this being a two-door car, she flipped the seat back to get a closer look at the figure inside.

"It's you!" she said. "Kris, what are you doing in this car? Were you out here all night? For heaven's sake, why didn't you tell me you didn't have a place to sleep? You could have frozen to death in there!"

I couldn't tell if she was angry with me or just frightened by the idea that a teenage girl could have died in her driveway. On the day after Christmas.

"Come on, sit up," she coaxed. "We've got to get you out of there."

She had to push and pull me along because I could barely move my body. I was shaking with chills, or was it fever? Bev, Kathy's mom, half-carried me inside. After I had been in there for 10 minutes of thawing out and sipping hot chocolate, she said, "We've got to get you to the hospital." I allowed her to usher me into her car, which was already heated, and we started slowly down the snow and ice-crusted street.

"It's pneumonia, and her fever is pretty severe," the emergency room doctor declared. "We're going to have to keep her here for a couple of days."

I wasn't going to argue with that, and I settled into a deep sleep that lasted at least 18 hours. Even after I woke up, I was in and out of sleep, feeling foggy, for at least another day before finally clearing out the cobwebs.

"Kris, don't worry about where you're going to go from here," Bev told me. "You're going to come home with me and stay with us, until Children's Services can figure out what to do."

Stay with us, spend the day I must. Lunch with the Brady Bunch. I stopped trying to follow my cloudy thoughts and drifted back to sleep.

The Conaways lived in what seemed to me like a huge home. It had a formal living room and a big family room too. The downstairs included a kitchen and two large bedrooms, with two more bedrooms upstairs. The kids were set up in three of the bedrooms, with Bev and her husband Gary sleeping in the master bedroom, just off the living room. She made a place for me on the pullout sofa in the living room, which meant I would be no more than 25 feet from her during the night.

From my first night there, I had never felt so safe. When she came out to check on my coughing and give me my medicine during the night, I had a sense of being deeply cared for, an experience I had never had in my life. If I really had come close to dying that night in the car, this woman had rescued me.

Bev pulled a couple of books off the built-in bookshelves in the family room and handed them to me to read. They were popular psychology books, something about growing up and entering adulthood. I didn't really read them much, but I was touched that she had given me something that she thought could help me.

January passed, and February too, and somewhere along the way it became clear, without much spoken about it, that Children's Services had made my friend Kathy's mother and father my temporary foster parents. Just until something more permanent was found, of course. I had no objection to that plan, none at all, and I began to get to know Kathy's siblings, two of whom were somewhere around the teen years like me, with the other two much younger. They welcomed me into their home, and I felt cozier and cozier in my little bed in the living room.

I almost forgot that I could never afford to get too comfortable anywhere because I never stayed in one place long. Sure enough, one day Bev informed me that Children's Services had decided on a placement for me: a school and living facility for emotionally troubled girls, operated partly by nuns. The name she referred to was Villa St. Rose, but to me it just came out "Christie School."

"I'm going backwards!" I said to myself, except that this place was a notch further up the scale of serious treatment because, unlike Christie School, Villa St. Rose was a fully locked-down facility.

As Bev drove me up toward the old school in north Portland, I could tell that she was impressed. The grounds were well-kept and attractive, just like most of the facilities I had been in, and when they brought us inside she saw beautiful antique furniture. "Ah, but she doesn't really know what I know about places like this," I said to myself. Then I had the thought: *maybe I can do something about that.*

When the neatly dressed woman meeting with us announced that, gosh, they did have a bed available and I could move in within a matter of days, I seized my chance.

"Can we have a tour first?" I asked.

"Well, actually, we don't usually provide tours here," she said, looking at Bev, not me. "We need to respect the privacy of the other girls. I'm sure you can understand."

I figured that would be the end of that idea and Bev would bring me home to get my stuff and drag me right back down here to set up my new life. I figured wrong.

"Oh, I think a tour would be a great idea," Bev said. "I wonder if that's something you can arrange for us, in a way that doesn't disturb the other girls or infringe on their privacy, of course."

The woman didn't blink, but just sat there for a long moment without answering. *That's right, Bev. You need to see what's behind those doors!*

"Let me see what I can do," the woman said, no doubt thinking of the cost of holding that open bed with my name on it. Soon she was back, dangling a set of those big keys. She opened the first metal doors and closed it behind us. *Clunk.*

It didn't take Bev long to discover that behind that pretty exterior lived some pretty hardened, scary looking girls. I could see her taking in the sight of the caged windows and soaking up the rigid, hospital environment. She might have come to this place carrying images from those cute movies that depict girls all living happily together in an orphanage, each with their own cozy beds neatly lined up in a row. That's the kind of place she wanted to leave me at. Now those images were snuffed out.

"Can we see the outside grounds?" I asked eagerly. The greeter who was now functioning as our tour guide allowed us only a brief glance out there, but it was enough for Bev to glimpse the fences with the barbed wire on top. *Hope she's thinking what I'm thinking.* We had barely climbed back into Bev's car when she turned to face me.

"You are NOT going to live in that place," she announced.

"No?" I asked innocently. I had wanted her to be shocked, and it seemed as if the tour had accomplished the mission.

"No way," she said. "If you go in there, we will lose you forever."

Cray Cray

I felt like, for the first time in my life, I had truly been saved. I liked the feeling.

I'm not sure how, but somehow Bev and Gary were granted approval to keep me long-term. I think it helped that they had a bit of a foster care resume, having performed that service for two children when they were living in New Mexico several years earlier. The way I imagined it, the state was making a statement that sounded something like this: "Fine, we don't know what else to do with this kid. She's blown up every other placement. Go ahead, give it a shot. And good luck!" I didn't mind the how's and why's. The only thing that mattered was that I had become this kind, caring woman's full-fledged, state-approved foster child.

I still have the pictures from my 15th birthday party that April. Bev baked me a birthday cake and handed me two presents: a pink cowl neck sweater with a stripe of cream that came down the shoulders, and a teal blue embroidered cotton shirt. They were both popular styles, they were both beautiful, and they both fit me perfectly. And the entire Conaway family treated my birthday as a special day, as if I really did belong there with them.

I had found myself a home. Of course, I still had to go to school. And whenever school and I ran into each other, trouble usually followed. I got caught smoking cigarettes and was kicked out briefly for that. Another day I got ahold of some marijuana, and after getting myself good and high, I took a walk during class time. When I spotted my new "sister" Kathy in her class, I made a big scene of waving to her. Her teacher did not appreciate my friendly appearance.

"Mademoiselle, come back here," he said as he stepped out of his classroom and began following me down the corridor. I answered in the spirit I always displayed when someone in authority was objecting to my behavior. "Fuck you!" I screamed, and when he still kept pursuing me and finally grabbed me by the shoulders, my automatic response button clicked on. I smacked him with my open hand, more of a scratch than a hard blow, but enough to draw blood. "Uh-oh," I said to myself. "Time to run." I wound up sitting on the toilet of a closed stall in the girls' bathroom, with my feet up, pressed against the door to block it.

I'm going to get thrown out of Bev's house for this, I thought, and I didn't budge when the teacher and assistant principal tried to lure me out. Then I heard another voice, softer and more feminine.

"It's okay, baby, you can come out," Bev said. "We'll take care of this."

And that's what she did. After a one-minute stopover in the principal's office, Bev had me alone with her in the car.

"You're just not ready to be in school," she explained. "You're going to stay home with me for a while. And I'm not going to let you get ten feet out of my sight."

As lunchtime approached on my first morning with my stay-at-home mom, she told me that she was going to show me how to make chef salad. She took out a real salad bowl with the wooden tongs and guided me through the operation. Then she laid out a linen tablecloth and brought fresh iced tea and plates to the table. "This is so fancy," I said to myself, "and so cool."

After the most enjoyable suspension I had ever had, I went back to school and apologized to that teacher whose face I had clawed. Things were going along calmly for a while, but I didn't like being told that my earlier trouble meant that I would not be allowed to attend the ninth-grade graduation dance to be held the day after the final day of school. "It's not fair!" I snapped to Bev, and I expected her to give me a big lecture about needing to face the consequences for my actions. You know, take the school's side. Once again, I underestimated her.

"This is absolutely unacceptable," she argued to the administrators when she marched back into school with me. "Kris has already paid the price for her actions. She needs to go to this dance."

Wow, how cool was this—having a mother willing to fight for me! And she won, too. The school relented and said I could go to the dance. Of course, I owed Bev a major debt of gratitude and should have been looking for every possible way to express it, right? Well, I hadn't quite learned that part of the mother-daughter relationship yet, unfortunately.

Cray Cray

It all began with spending the money I had saved to buy tickets for the AC/DC concert in Portland on the night of the final day of school. Kathy was going to go with me, along with a few boys from school. Bev had approved that plan, but I didn't stop there. I figured that since it was the last day of school, we really didn't need to be in class. To get into the spirit of the day and night to come, we should go off and party all day instead. Kathy had a migraine that morning and stayed home, but I still hustled off to my friend Jeff's house with the other two guys, Scott and Michael. Jeff had built something like a fort in the attic of his home, and with his mother off at work we thought that would be the perfect place to drink some booze and smoke some weed. That would get us in the right mood for the concert.

Bam, bam, bam! Someone was on to our party, and it didn't sound like it was one of the kids from school, jealous at not being invited.

"I know you're in there," she said. *Bev!* She was banging with a broom handle.

"No! I'm not coming down until I get good and high," I said between hits off the bong in front of me. But Bev was persistent, and the three boys made it clear they weren't ready to fight off any invaders. So, I lifted the little hatch door to the attic and came out.

"Follow me outside," Bev said firmly, but without raising her voice. Once she got me out to the driveway, she said, "You're not going to the concert tonight, but that will be your only consequence."

"Oh, no, I'm not missing that concert," I said. "It's AC/DC."

"Fine, then for every hour that you are gone, you will be grounded for one week of summer."

"I don't care. I'm still going! Just leave me alone."

I think I surprised her with my unwillingness to accept her generous terms. But she didn't really know just how much of a fighter I had become, how much of a bad-ass I really was. It was an identity that I could not easily leave behind.

"Oh, just come home, baby," she said as she followed me in little loops around the edge of the driveway. That's when she fell, and when she landed she began sobbing. I knew that she wasn't hurt, physically at least. I should have come right to her side and apologized and told her I would stop acting that way, but I was too confused and scared and a whole bunch of other things I didn't understand.

"Just get up," I said sternly. "People are going to see you. You're embarrassing me." And when she forced herself up off the ground and said again that I "should just come home," I dug in even more firmly.

"Fuck you! I'm not going anywhere with *you!*" I yelled. She swiped at her nose with her hand. I could see that she was struggling for what to say and do next.

"Well, then...well, f-f-fuck you too!" she finally blurted out.

With the way that she turned away from me and marched down the street, her head held low, I was sure that this was the first time Bev had ever spoken the "f" word out loud. That's how far I had driven this woman who had demonstrated time and again how deeply she cared for me, and how willing she was to stand up for me and my chance at a life outside of a jail cell or a loony bin.

I went to the AC/DC concert, but I didn't feel triumphant. I was absolutely, totally miserable. More important, I did not run away. I fully accepted the sentence handed down by my new parental authority, and I did not tear down the calendar posted on our refrigerator that had the word "Grounded" written across it each week for all of summer vacation. It wasn't such a harsh penalty anyway. I was allowed to have friends over to the house, and we would sit for hours talking on the soft lawn of the Conaways' front yard. Not only that, I could eat anything I wanted, watch TV as long as I chose, and I had moved off the pull-out sofa in the living room and relocated in what had been Bev's sewing room. I had my own room! It felt so powerful to have my own space. My furnishings included two wooden apple crates to hold my few personal belongings, including my own curling iron and hair dryer that I got on my own—I never did get that blow dryer my mother promised me for

Christmas. I even had a small dresser and a window that allowed me to look outside. I felt so safe, and so at home.

Bev also helped steer me toward a volunteer job through the CETA (Comprehensive Employment and Training Act) program that had been launched by President Nixon a few years earlier. I served as a classroom aide at the Edwards Center, helping adults with developmental disabilities. Mostly I sat with the men and women there and assisted them in doing puzzles or other simple learning tasks. I loved this work because I was actually helping other people.

Yes, penalty or not, it was a very good summer. I remember only one day that summer when things were not so warm and cozy. The Conaways had rented the movie *One Flew Over the Cuckoo's Nest* and played it on their VCR. I knew that this was the movie filmed at the Oregon State Hospital, but it was a family social time and I tried to watch. When I recognized the character of McMurphy's psychiatrist as the actual superintendent of the hospital, someone I had seen right inside my old home, I had to run out of the family room and high-tail it up to my sewing room.

"Kris, what made you so upset?" Bev asked when she came up a while later.

Why? That place, those people, that horrible environment you're watching in some movie, that's all real to me. That place traumatized me! I can't stand to see it. I don't want to remember.

Those were the words I could have shared, if I had already grown into that kind of awareness and understanding back then. But that would not happen for quite a long time. In reality, when Bev asked me that question I didn't say one word...

Kathy and I began spending more and more time together. I wasn't the best influence on her, of course. I got her to start smoking marijuana with me, and we got so bold smoking near the house, or inside the house when her parents were out, that one day I left my water pipe sitting in the middle of the dining room. It was still there the next morning when we all sat down to eat breakfast, but the next day it was gone. I guess

Bev and her husband just needed to make a statement. When we were stoned, and even when we weren't, Kathy and I would talk about our hopes and dreams for the lives ahead of us. I don't remember the details, except that for the first time I was able to imagine myself in a positive and rewarding situation. Oh, and I would definitely travel a lot. Maybe someday I'd even go to Russia—for real, not in my imagined journeys as the Babushka when I was a lost and neglected little girl. I was beginning to grow up and allowing myself to feel that this could be something normal, maybe even something good. I was even earning some money with some neighborhood babysitting jobs that Kathy and I landed.

Ah, the babysitting money. That was the subject of the argument that Kathy and I got into one afternoon. I was convinced that something about our little arrangement was not fair, and when Kathy did not immediately agree with me, I took exception to her position. And when I tried to use my words, to express my feelings appropriately like I had been taught in the state hospital, and she still didn't come around, well, I did something else that I had learned to do in my days as the crazy girl. I got up close to her and gave her a hard shove, sending her toppling back against the wall and down onto the floor. Thud!

Bev was not home that day, but my foster father Gary was. The noise brought him immediately to the scene, and after making sure that Kathy was not really hurt, although obviously shaken by my little display of aggression, he turned to me. Grabbing hold of me, he pulled me a safe distance from his daughter and said, "No! You are not going to do that here. We do not tolerate that kind of behavior in this house."

In that moment, I just panicked. I had blown it! There I was, safe and cozy in the most loving and caring home I had ever known, with people who accepted me and treated me like a decent and worthy human being, and I had screwed it up. Now I was going to get kicked out of the house, and I would never have another chance like this as long as I lived.

"Fuck you!" I screamed. Racing to the front door, a solid wood door, I kicked and kicked until it split open. But I was not going to be content with just running down the road and never looking back. Nope, not the bad-ass girl. I headed next to the garage door, with the little windows on the upper half. *Bam! Bam! Bam!* I punched every one of those windows out, cutting myself up so badly in the process that I still have the scars to show for it.

"Fuck you!" I screeched again. "I'm out of here! I'm never coming back to this family. I don't need you, I don't need any of you! I'm going off on my own. I'll be just fine, you'll see."

Only then, after my last violent and profane scene, was I ready to exit stage left. The wild girl, the real bad-ass, had managed to live for nine months in this peaceful, caring home and family. She had stayed warm and safe, protected inside the womb. But now, the time had arrived for her to come bursting out into the world—ready or not!

10
A Kid in Grown-up's Clothing

I had no plan, no blueprint for self-survival. My only thought as I trudged off from the home of the Conaways, my own foster family, was to walk the two blocks to Scott's house. Scott was one of the boys in the attic fort where we got caught partying on the last day of school, and he had visited me often when I held court on Bev's front lawn during my summer of being grounded.

I couldn't stop crying. I had just blown the best deal of my life, although in my mind I believed I had no choice. As a 15-year-old girl, I didn't have the awareness to put all the pieces together, but if I had been able to sort out the bloody, broken-window, busted-door picture left in my wake, it would have looked something like this:

When you finally get something you have never had, and you grasp more clearly just how much you had been living without, it can be excruciating. In some hard-to-understand way, it was scary for me to be loved and cared for like that. Somehow, not consciously, I just couldn't tolerate it. I also could not escape the belief that as a foster child, even in such a kind and loving family, I would always be their last choice. If we were all in a boat together in the ocean and got caught in a terrible storm and somebody had to be dumped overboard so the others could survive, it would be me getting tossed into the raging sea. That's the reality that was driving me when I shoved my sister and my dad said, "We do not tolerate this kind of behavior in this house." My wild girl popped in because what I heard him saying between words was, "We have to get rid of you!" Better for me to say fuck you to him, and to the whole family, so I could cling to some sense that I was choosing to leave, that I was in control. Internally, I probably knew that I couldn't control all of my ingrained impulses anyway, so even if I survived this outburst I would just create another incident and that would be the end for sure. So, I took myself out before they could...

Scott wasn't home, but somebody was there to let me in. Without stopping to explain, I made a beeline for the phone. Picking up the phone book, I frantically searched for the number of Children's Services. I had to call Cecily. *Stop crying*, I thought. *You can't be crying when you talk to Cecily.*

"I can't stay at that home anymore," I told my case worker. "I just want to be on my own." As I described the blow-up scene, Cecily seemed to be listening closely. Amazingly, she didn't argue with my decision.

"Well, there is no other place for you to go now anyway," she said finally. "So, if you are that determined to live on your own, I will try to look the other way...for a while. But, Kristy, you have to stay out of trouble. If you get yourself in any trouble, if you do something violent or against the law, you'll go to Hillcrest (a girls' criminal maximum-security facility). That's the future you would be looking at."

I gulped. "Oh, don't worry, I won't get in any trouble," I said firmly. To myself, I was saying, "I might have to do things that some people would consider wrong, but I just won't get caught doing it. I do not want to be locked up again. I won't let that happen."

So, I had my ticket to ride. Now I just had to figure out where to go. At first, I had no idea who to turn to, but then a name popped into my mind: David. He was a guy several years older than me that I had become friends with during my summer of volunteering at the Edwards Center.

"Can I stay with you, just for a while until I get this all figured out?"

I asked him. David was 24 and taking classes at Portland Community College to learn the skills needed to become a small engine mechanic. Since I could be very persuasive when in need, he soon agreed to help me. I reached out to Bev to inform her where I would be staying, and she was kind enough to bring me a bag of my personal belongings at our agreed meeting point: a Denny's restaurant across the street from David's apartment complex. When my mom saw me, she didn't give me any lectures about what had happened with her husband. It was true that Gary had been somewhat ambivalent about accepting me as a foster child, but I knew that she backed him up in telling me that I had crossed the line. But as she always had done with me, she looked for the positive.

"Kris, I really believe you have the capacity to live independently," she said. "You can do this! And we'll keep in touch."

The part of me that wanted more than anything to go back, to return to the safety of the womb, was calling up some tears. But the part of me that was determined to make it my way choked them off. I had to live my life.

That meant that even though I had a place, with a friend who was becoming more of a boyfriend, I had to get a job. Because I was not yet 16, I was limited to workplaces that did not require a work permit. The CETA program was not available now because my job working with people with developmental disabilities was only a summer volunteer arrangement for teens. CETA was geared to assist needy adults in the job market. I lied about my age to score a job at one restaurant, but after a couple of weeks and a paycheck or two, they discovered the truth and gave me the boot. Dang it! By then I was already contributing money to help support my new shared household, and instead of telling David that I had lost my source of income, I just turned to another way to bring home some money. At least I had company sitting on the brick wall in the 4th and Clay district of Portland, with other girls doing their best to drum up business.

To bring in additional resources, I also decided to apply for Food Stamps.

I understood that only adults were eligible to receive this government assistance, but rather than lie about my age, I just stated my case.

"I'm a ward of the state. They're my legal guardians," I explained. "I think the state should at least give me food stamps to help me live."

The woman processing my application didn't know what to say to that reasoning, and after a meeting with three or four supervisors and a call to Cecily, she just shrugged her shoulders and authorized my application. I had hit the jackpot—$57 per month in Food Stamps! I was thrilled to be making my own little grocery list, purchasing my own box of Cap'n Crunch cereal and bringing in a steady supply of blueberry yogurt and huge blocks of cheddar cheese. I even helped to prepare dinners of spaghetti and beef stroganoff for David and I.

Determined to leave behind my sex-for-survival routine, I put up notes on all the doors of our apartment complex looking for cleaning jobs. Immediately, I was approached by two guys who needed someone to pick up their apartment after their weekend parties. When the evidence left behind pointed to heavy use of cocaine, I just reminded myself that they were paying me well. I must have been doing a good job for them because they soon approached me with another money-making opportunity.

"Do you know how to drive?" they asked me. Well, I didn't have a driver's license, but when I was living with Bev I had talked friends into letting me drive around with them in their parents' cars. Sure, I could drive. "We need you to go to Portland and drop off a package for us," they informed me.

So, there I was in a shiny red Camaro, with a stick shift, hitting the gas and launching my mission with a loud vroom! My destination was the parking lot of a Plaid Pantry convenience store in southeast Portland. It felt so powerful driving that swanky car through the tunnel heading toward downtown. After I arrived, I waited and waited for the rendezvous person to arrive. I didn't even see him coming, so his sudden presence at my window scared the bejesus out of me.

"Okay, girl, I'm here to pick up the package," he said, and I immediately handed it out to him through the window. Proud of how I had handled my job, I took the scenic route home. When I reported back, I was paid with a fifty-dollar bill. Wow! I was only getting ten bucks per "event" in my other Portland work. This new employment had real potential in my mission to live an independent life. I was eagerly awaiting my next assignment from my two neighbors.

Bam, bam, bam! A few days later, my two bosses arrived at David's apartment in the morning, while he was at school. They were pissed.

"Where is it?" the bigger guy asked when I opened the door. When he pushed his coat aside, I could see that he was carrying a firearm.

"Where's what?" I asked innocently.

"The package! You had a delivery to make for us, and you didn't make it."

"What? No, I gave it to that guy, just like you told me to do."

"You've got it! We know you've got it. Where is it?"

So that package must have had something valuable inside.

"I don't know what you're talking about," I insisted, and after the confrontation went on for a minute, I told them I had to go to the bathroom. They watched me go down the hall.

Now what am I going to do? I thought after I closed the bathroom door. *I can't get in any trouble—I promised Cecily. And those guys…they could kill me!* That's when the plan came to me. When I was sure they were not watching, I hopped out of the bathroom to the bedroom across the hall. *David keeps a gun in here, a 30 ought 6 if I recall. I think it was over there in the corner.*

Yes, that gun was still there. Moving quickly, I burst toward the living room, trying to summon every ounce of my bad-ass bravado.

"Get out of here, Motherfuckers, or I'll blow you away!" I screamed, and when they froze in place, I added, "I fucking mean it!" When the bigger guy reached toward his pocket, I fired my weapon—not toward my employers but into the wall. It was close enough to accomplish the task, however. They were gone in a flash.

I didn't pause to consider the possibility that I could have hurt or even killed someone. All I knew was that the police were going to be coming and that if they picked me up I was going to jail, maybe forever. I dropped the gun, grabbed my little bag that I kept some of my stuff in and rushed across the street to the Denny's where I had met Bev.

"Kathy, you've got to come over to Denny's, right now!" I said when my foster sister answered the phone. After I explained what had happened, she was on her way, with no hard feelings about that shoving incident that led to my banishment from my foster home.

"You've got to tell Mom," Kathy urged when we sat down together with our coffee at Denny's.

"Oh, no, no, no," I said. "We're not calling Mom. I can't get in any trouble. I just have to figure out how not to get caught by the police. And I'm worried about David. He's going to be furious. It's his home." I cared about this man who had taken me in, and I wanted to explain what had happened. I also wanted more of my belongings for wherever I was going to go next.

Kathy and I kept peeking outside to watch for signs of the police. When I was sure that the coast was clear, she and I hurried to the apartment. David had gotten home from school.

"What have you done?" he shouted. I had never seen him so angry. "They evicted me, I've got to be out in 72 hours!"

After I explained the whole story and told him that I was scared those two guys were going to come looking for me, David began to calm down. He even agreed to drive me to Portland in his green and white VW bus. I lied that I had a friend to stay with, and since I knew I couldn't ask him to drop me at 4th and Clay, I directed him to leave me at a very familiar getaway spot: The Park Blocks.

Now what I am going to do? I slept in some bushes under a big tree to ward off the rain. The next morning, I asked some of the homeless adults about where I could find a shelter to take me in. "You're not old enough—if you go to a shelter the people there might turn you in,"

Cray Cray

I was told. And I knew they were right. Then I thought of the cheap hotels in the seedy section of the city. Of course, I would need some quick money to afford a room even at a place like that. So it was more sex-for-survival until I had put together about sixty bucks, which got me three nights at a place on 82nd Street that was so dirty and smelly that I used towels to make little pathways through the room so my feet wouldn't have to touch the floor. On my first night, I bought a sandwich at the nearest 7-Eleven and tried to summon the nerve to call my mother. No, not Bev, my birth mother.

"Can I come back home...I mean, like, just for a few days?" I asked.

"Absolutely not," she said. "But I'll tell you what. If you come up here, I'll buy you lunch."

I got on the bus and I met my mother at the same Chinese restaurant that she used to take me to during her binging runs. She wasn't eating when I got there, just drinking her 7 and 7's. True to her word, she did buy me lunch. But she did not change her mind about allowing me to come back to her home for a few nights, and she certainly was not offering me any money. And yet this woman who had neglected and abandoned me, and who couldn't even commit to making visits to see me at the state hospital, made one of the most supportive gestures she had ever extended to me.

"You need a real job, and I'll help you get one," she said. "There's a Burger King nearby. I'll drive you right over there now and you can apply. You can use my address and phone number for a contact on your application."

Soon, my intoxicated mother was driving me to the Burger King, and the next day they called her to announce that I had an interview appointment. When I rode the bus up from Portland and arrived on time, I was hired on the spot. I smiled, not just to have acquired an "honest job" but because not so long ago I had tried to talk my way into a job at McDonald's and got turned away. Now I was making my fast-food breakthrough at Burger King.

I dressed up in my little uniform, with the brown pants and orange and yellow shirt with the brown stripes, and the little hat. I was assigned to run the beverage station, back at a time when the employees filled customers' drinks instead of them doing it themselves in the eating area. My pay was $4 an hour, but I was promised a raise up to $4.05 in a short time if I proved myself worthy. And, aside from one little incident with a difficult customer, I aced the test. I had become a legitimate working girl. I even created my own little breakfast when it was time for our free meal by taking some ham they used for ham sandwiches and putting it in the fryer, then placing it on a long roll with lettuce and tomato—something like a BLT.

To support this new employment, I had to find a place to live. That's where David, my ever-loyal and supportive boyfriend, stepped up by agreeing to cosign for a lease agreement for my very own apartment. I was really starting to get the hang of this independent living thing! Of course, I did sometimes need to supplement my income with sex-for-survival. I also visited the Food Bank once a month.

This new arrangement was working okay for a while, but with a $205 rent payment due each month, the financial strain of keeping my own place was proving too severe. Soon I met a young woman in the apartment complex who lost her roommate and invited me to replace her. She even had horses and took me riding once.

So many things were falling into place that I barely noticed the quiet passing of my 16th birthday, totally unlike the year before when Bev and my foster family made the day so special. Bev did keep in touch, as promised, and she continued to cheer me on from afar and invited me over for holidays. I knew that she loved me, but I also realized that there was no going back. I was on my own and I was going to continue to figure out how to make it.

As much as I appreciated the stability of my job at Burger King, I knew that I would have to set my sights higher. I still believed I could get something through CETA again. Sure, you were supposed to be an adult to qualify for their job training positions, but I had talked my away into getting Food Stamps when I wasn't an adult, hadn't I? So, I visited the CETA office and made the same case: "I'm a ward of the state so the government should help me do what I need to do to get by." No dice. Undaunted, I decided to come back to the CETA office a second time—after changing my hair and general appearance, and altering the name on my application from my stepfather's last name to the last name I carried from birth. I also declared that I was 18 years old.

"Hmm, weren't you in here the other day?" the woman at the window asked.

"What? What are you talking about?" I said. "No, no, uh-uh. I've never been here before."

I can't say for sure that she totally believed me. Anyway, since I had made the commitment to live on my own, I just seemed to be running into situations where people were willing to look the other way when I was trying to take some new step to keep me off the streets. Although I was still a kid, I was dressing up in adult's clothing. I was making a statement, and somehow that made others take me seriously.

I was accepted into a CETA program to provide training in non-traditional jobs for women. For four months, I was going to learn to operate heavy equipment. Not only was the training free, but I would be getting a small stipend to help meet living expenses, a critical benefit since I had to quit my wonderful job at Burger King in order to qualify for this program as an unemployed "adult."

As part of our training, we also were placed in classes at Portland Community College, where we learned resume writing, interviewing and other basic skills. I handled the classroom instruction fine, and I loved going out for on-the-job training at work sites. Wearing our boots and hard hats, we women all looked tough. Guys who did this sort of thing for a living split us into groups of four and taught us how to handle backhoes, cranes and other impressive equipment. I was gung-ho about our prospects at first, but after a few days, we began to get a strong message about how we would be "welcomed" on real construction jobs when we got through the training. Catcalls, insults, snide remarks, dirty looks. After my experience in another line of work that placed me in regular contact with men who didn't exactly respect and value women, this was not going to cut it for me. In the end, only a handful of women in our program passed through the gate and earned jobs in this man's world.

Now what am I going to do? Almost immediately I had an idea: college! Sure, I had never even gotten close to a high school degree, but I had held my own in those classes at Portland Community College. I could go to college, earn a degree and find a real-paying job. Yep, I could do that.

"Um, you do realize that going to school here costs money, right?" I was told the day I walked into the community college's admissions office eager to sign up for classes. Actually, I never even thought of that. The classes I had taken there before were covered by a government program, but now I was going to have to be a paying student. I got an application for financial aid, and when they told me I would need to fill in information regarding my parents' financial situation, I realized that Bev and her husband's status could sabotage my chances of qualifying for assistance from the school. And my foster parents were not offering to pay my way.

Once again, I managed to convince someone to bend the rules in my favor, submitting my own financial info that referenced my meager income from Burger King. That's how I earned enough financial aid to become a college girl. Now I just needed a job to keep me afloat.

I approached the Edwards Center seeking work directly through them, rather than as part of any CETA program. By now, I was 17. Since I had proven myself in my earlier position there, I was awarded a job at a group home. I would be working the overnight shift, taking care of the adults living there and sleeping when I could. Once again, I embraced the chance to actually help people who needed it.

Soon I had a routine: four nights a week, I would arrive at Edwards Center at 7 p.m. and work there until 7 or 8 in the morning. Then I would drive to school and attend classes during the day before going back to my shared apartment for at best a couple of hours of sleep until I had to head off to work. On weekends, I would hang out with David. I had a very busy life, and I was NOT getting into any trouble. Of course,

Cray Cray

most of the time I was totally exhausted. But I was determined to make it all work, and I took great pride in earning A's in my first round of remedial classes. Not bad for a girl whose third-grade report card was filled with D's.

Yes, I was really living like a responsible adult now in all kinds of arenas, including personal relationships. David had given me an engagement ring, and I was proud to wear it. I knew that he cared for me deeply, not even bolting when I fired a gun in his apartment and got him evicted, and I had to admit that I had begun to care about his welfare, too. David drank, a lot, and after living with my alcoholic mother and at times staying with my alcoholic grandmother, I believed that I understood the signs. I made an appointment with a counselor at Catholic Community Services, and after explaining my boyfriend's behavior she nodded and said, "From what you're telling me, he does have a drinking problem." She handed me a little pamphlet about AA, and when I gave it to David, along with my little speech about how I believed he needed help and that I would stand by him while he got it, he instantly agreed.

David began attending AA meetings, and I did my part by going to Al-Anon. I was very talkative in my group, and after I happened to mention that I smoked marijuana fairly often and that I had messed around with LSD and mushrooms, one of the attendees who had been around awhile gave me a stern look. "I think you're in the wrong room," she said. "You need to be over there in those AA meetings."

That's exactly what I did. I joined David in AA and NA, attending at least five meetings a week with him, and I totally quit any and all drug use. I don't believe that I was actually an addict, but I stuck around because I loved the community of people committed to improving their lives and supporting one another along the way. It was the kind of community where if you didn't show up, people noticed, and wanted to know why. It was also helpful to discover that while I had definitely gone through some tough times already, other people had it rough, too. Almost every meeting, I would hear another story that touched me and encouraged me to keep doing what I had to do to live the right way. I always felt uplifted in the presence of those who showed up at those 12-step meetings.

It was during one of those uplifting moments when I happened to notice the person sitting across from me. "Wow, who are you?" I said silently. I was instantly drawn to this person and after that meeting I was not at all shy about making my move—even though I was engaged to marry my boyfriend, and even though this other person happened to be a woman. As it turned out, she felt the same magnetic pull. That meant that I had come face to face with another adult situation. By this time, David's mother was already well along in planning her son's wedding.

"David, we've got a situation," I began when we got home from an NA meeting a couple of weeks later. "I've got a big crush on this girl. I think I might be, I don't know, gay, or bisexual…or something."

Once again, he remained calm. I had been living with the sweetest boyfriend in the world.

"Well, I guess we better call off the engagement then," he said.

"Yeah, I guess we better," I said sadly.

And that's how I began an intense romantic relationship with Ann, a woman a few years older than me who had an infant girl. I was head over heels with Ann, and I soon fell in love with her daughter Sarah too. Ann and I were lovingly accepted as a couple by our AA community, and we were determined to make our relationship work. Of course, we were not free from other kinds of adult issues and challenges.

For starters, the full-time work, full-time student grind sometimes wore me down. The truth was, I was in and out of community college and was eventually fired from my job at the Edwards Center for being insubordinate with my supervisor. And Ann faced her own struggles. Ann's parents provided stability and sustenance for Sarah while we worked towards stabilizing.

When money was tight, we lived in the back of the Toyota Corolla that I paid $800 for, and we tracked every free food giveaway we could find: grocery store samples, Saturday afternoon hot dogs in a car dealer's showroom, whatever. Sometimes after Ann got off work in the morning we'd drive up to Sauvie Island and sleep on the beach. Eventually we got the nerve to approach a family homeless shelter.

"We are partners and want to be housed together," I said to the intake coordinator. She stared at us awhile, shuffled some papers, went to a back room to talk to the director and finally showed us to our room. Keep in mind this was about 1982, back in the days when same-sex couples were not exactly showered with rights and privileges. Once again, I had boldly stood up for myself and a door had been opened, rules or no rules.

We set ourselves on a course together, taking on every difficulty that showed up on our path. I got a new job with another residential treatment facility for adults with developmental disabilities, and Ann worked the night shift at Dunkin' Donuts. Before long we had obtained a low-income-housing apartment, and Sarah joined us full-time again. So now I added full-time co-parenting to my responsibilities. And I was so determined to do it right, to avoid all those mistakes that I had suffered. Of course, I had lots of lessons to learn, especially in the area of unrealistic expectations. When the 18-month-old child of the household decided it would be great fun to throw food off her high chair, I would swoop in and declare, "No, no, you have to stop that!" It took a while to realize that a good parent does not get worked up over normal little kid behavior. But I was determined, and slowly I began letting go of my rookie parent mistakes.

On my 18th birthday, when I was officially ushered into the world of adulthood, Ann gave me a plastic heart with "LOVE" printed on it. I did have love in my life, and I had begun to learn to take the fighting spirit that helped me survive as a child and adolescent and apply it to all the adult-world challenges in my path. I was trying so hard to prove to myself and everyone around me that I was not crazy, that I was not only a normal person but a *good* person, a responsible and reliable person, someone who also could do good for other people in this world. I was going to get a real education, find meaningful and well-paying work and create and sustain a happy, loving, stable family.

That's what everyone wants, right? Shouldn't I be able to have that too? Just because my entire childhood had delivered blow after blow of pain, suffering, hardship, rejection and loss, that didn't mean that I should want or expect anything less than what everyone else was after.

That's the belief I fought to hold onto. Unfortunately, I also had to confront the reality that my launching point for shooting for the stars was much, much lower than others. My past was not yet ready to release me from its haunting, burning grasp. That didn't mean that I could never achieve my goals for a fulfilling life. It just meant that it was going to be a very steep climb, that it might take longer than I was hoping, and that before I could soar up into the stratosphere I just might have to plunge back down into the fire.

11

Hand on the Telephone

Sometimes we never know when and why the dark clouds descend upon us. Often the best we can do after we get caught in the storm is just try to ride it out. Retracing our footsteps to see how we got there, and why, comes later.

The swirling winds of despair hit me right after I was put under to have my wisdom teeth removed. Almost as soon as the anesthesia wore off, I found myself in the midst of a severe depressive episode. I couldn't function, could hardly even get out of bed. And suddenly, everything about my life seemed dark, dismal, hopeless. I could barely summon enough energy to grab my journal now and then to capture what was happening.

Pain, pain, the pain inside my head. My skin crawls, my bones ache, my head explodes.

My feelings scared me, and for the first time since I had taken the vow to live my life on my own, I began having serious thoughts of suicide. Thankfully, I was smart enough to reach out for help. I got myself to the emergency room, where they could easily determine that I was in need of immediate psychiatric care. Unfortunately, the hospital had no available beds in its psych unit, so I had to be transported to another facility. Even in my foggy state, I recognized the place right away: Cedar

Hills Hospital, my psychiatric pitstop between Christie School and Oregon State Hospital.

Something else looked very familiar when they wheeled me out of the ambulance. I noticed a truck parked on the street right in front of the hospital, with a man sitting in it. It was my birth father. In what world does this happen…I mean, really? When I was assigned to a room that looked directly out at his parking spot, I soon figured out that he wasn't there to visit. He was living in that truck, and he had chosen the surroundings of Cedar Hills Hospital as his home. By then I had uncovered enough pieces about my childhood to understand that my father was dealing with untreated bipolar disorder.

So, as I began to get to know my fellow patients, I had a lot to talk about.

"See that homeless man living in his truck out there?" I would say. "That's my daddy. No, really, my father lives in that truck."

Other times I would raise eyebrows when I would tell the others, "I was here before, you know. Yeah, but I was only 12 years old then. Oh, and they took us on an outing to a rock concert once and I got drunk for the first time in my life and then I got sent to Oregon State Hospital right after they made *One Flew Over the Cuckoo's Nest* there…"

I had been plunked down in front of a window into my past, and the scene was not pretty. Even after I was discharged from the hospital and sent home with Ann and Sarah, I could not let go of the images that had crept up. I didn't have any contact with my father during that hospital stay, but I learned from my biological sister Karen that after not spending any time in the Aloha area for years, he had recently shown up in her life. But he never made any effort to reach out to me. Suddenly, I felt a strong sense that I had lost my father all over again. He had walked out of my life when I was four, and he was steering clear of me now. And, as I was told, his mental illness had more firmly taken hold. The active dad who used to take me ice skating and who taught me how to ride a bike was long gone. He was only a shell of himself.

The feeling that I could not stuff back down inside was that I had been cheated out of having a real father when I was young and vulnerable, when I really needed him. I had been cheated out of so much I had wanted back then.

She has her
And her has he
And all I have left is me.

That little poem sprang up in my journal when I found myself reflecting on that short period of living with my mother, my stepfather and my sister, when each of them seemed to be getting something from the other while I was getting nothing but the label that I was the problem, that I was the cause of all their troubles, that I was unworthy to live with them, that I was crazy, that I had to be sent away to be fixed.

And what happened to me at all those places where I was supposed to be "fixed?"

Tile floor, hard and cold on my flesh. Clothes ripped off my small but chubby child body. Arms twisting behind my back, legs spread-eagled, face mashed to the side. Breathe in, breathe out. Count the breaths. Weight crushing me. The prick of the needle and the buzzing in my head...going limp. The violation is complete.

Those were the vivid details that I was recalling from those times when I was forcibly restrained at both Cedar Hills and Oregon State Hospital. I hadn't thought of those violations for years, but now they were back in my face. I couldn't ignore them. It was all rushing back, like torrential rains descending upon me from those dark storm clouds, and no shelter within reach.

While all this was happening in my individual world, in the larger world the AIDS epidemic had begun to take hold. One dear friend died after Ann and I had cared for him in our home during his final days, and another close friend, a co-worker of mine who was devoted to the helping profession, was also diagnosed with the disease. So was his wife.

With the earth beneath my feet beginning to crumble, I could no longer work. I stayed in bed more and more, getting up only in mid-afternoon before Sarah came home from school to scrounge up some simple dinner, watch an hour or two of TV and go right back to bed. Then the big earthquake struck: my relationship with Ann, which had rubbed up against its share of adult struggles, was ending. Not only that, but I was losing Sarah. By then I had come to regard her very much as my child, too, but since she was not mine by blood, and I was not legally married to her mother, I had no grounds to even gain visitation.

"You've failed...failed at being normal," I said to myself. "You don't have a real relationship, you don't have a real kid, you don't have real parents, you don't have real anything."

I wound up in a tiny, low-income housing apartment that I supplied with a bed, one dining table and one chair for my living room, all obtained at a furniture bank. I slept 16 hours a day and subsisted on two baloney sandwiches, one in the morning and one at night, made from meat and bread I purchased at the 7-Eleven around the corner. Once in a while I would manage to rise myself up from a prone position in bed to scribble words in my journal.

Bootstrapper, that's what they used to call me. I would keep pulling myself up by my bootstraps. Striving against all odds. But now my straps are stretched out. No more snapback. Get up, brush yourself off? No, can't play anymore. I'm just so tired.

At some point, I can't remember how, I dragged myself to the county mental health center. They were focusing on a program designed to reduce hospitalization stays by treating clients with severe problems with more frequent therapy sessions. I liked Lois, the therapist assigned to me. She was gentle with me and I did not feel judged by her at all. Unlike all my other experiences as a psychiatric patient, where I was expected to remain passive while the professional experts told me what was wrong, she took more of a humanistic, give-and-take approach with me. And she was able to show me that what I was suddenly going through, the storm surge building up around me, was actually a very normal response to the trauma I had experienced growing up. "Normal." I liked that word, wanted to make it fit.

I saw Lois frequently until she told me that she would soon be leaving the facility and moving away. *What? I'm losing someone else in my life?* I thought. But with the way that Lois handled the situation, I could not be angry or heartbroken. She told me that the clinical team had selected Diana as the right person to continue the therapeutic work with me, and rather than just say goodbye and leave me with Diana, Lois sat me in one of the small, windowless consultation rooms and said, "I'm going to get Diana now, and then we're all going to sit and talk together."

When Diana walked in, I noticed that she was older than Lois, with gray hair, but beautiful, with clear blue eyes. She was dressed in comfortable clothes: black skirt, sandals, light jacket. "She's kind of flowy," I said to myself. Diana shook my hand warmly and when she sat down, Lois began to tell her all about me and my history…right in front of me. Her tone was kind and respectful, and after mentioning some new piece to my puzzle, she would turn to me and say, "Is there anything you would add to that, Kris?"

With each new detail about my traumatic experiences, Diana would nod her head, open her eyes wide and say, "Wow!" *Wow is right*, I thought. When Lois reached the part of my story about being admitted to the Oregon State Hospital as a 12-year-old girl, Diana added more commentary after the "wow." Turning to me, she said, "I've never met anyone who was a patient in the state hospital as a child." As Lois continued to emphasize that I had a "very intense trauma history," Diana's expression seemed to match that intensity. I felt right away that she got me, that she understood that what I had gone through was big and had left a huge imprint on me. It was so reassuring to know that when I brought up all those things that had happened to me, I was not just making a big hoo-ha out of something that was common stuff, not worth the time and bother to think about or reflect upon.

I was totally comfortable with being handed off from Lois to Diana, and even more assured when they set up a brief initial schedule where I would see them on alternate sessions—with Lois providing me hands-on depression management and Diana delving more into my trauma. When Lois left, I began seeing Diana twice a week individually, along with participating in a therapy group.

I had somebody totally in my corner, somebody who was ready and willing to listen to me recount my experiences growing up in an unsafe home and then being dumped in environments that in many ways were even less safe. I had a lot to talk about: about neglect and abuse, about rejection and abandonment, about scary foster homes and dirty and stinky emergency shelters, and especially about institutional care. Yes, I was poked, prodded and pathologized, not to mention physically and sexually abused. And through it all, I wore the big label: CRAZY. I was still trying to wrestle myself free from that label now, and I was finding it to be an identity that stuck to my body and mind like flypaper.

"I want to be a good person, to be a part of society, but look at me. I can't even function," I would say. "There has to be something wrong with me."

"I think what's happening is that all your trauma from the past has caught up with you," Diana would say. "That's totally natural."

Yeah, well, it may have been natural, but that sure didn't mean that it felt good. Not with the nightmares and flashbacks, the words and actions that echoed over and over. I still couldn't get past the belief that with so many bad things that happened to me, and the way I had lashed out in my anger and defiance, I had to be bad. Yep, I was a bad seed. I was still stuck with the habit of pathologizing my behavior. It was what had been routinely stuffed into my brain by many people, in so many places, for a long, long time.

Diana suggested that my violent, impulsive displays simply illustrated my need to act out. She's the one that first explained to me how, in my child's way, I was trying to bring attention to what was happening, first in my family and then later in psychiatric care facilities. I was trying to tell my story, to communicate to anyone who would listen that something was really wrong. And the more it seemed as if nobody was really listening, the more dramatically I acted out.

"You were never a crazy kid," Diana would say. She also tried to help me reframe what my parents and my stepfather had done. They did not take me away to somewhere where I could get better, as they kept insisting. They had given me away, like an unwanted pet being dumped by the side of the road with the vague idea that somebody might pick it up and take it home or bring it to a shelter.

"Any child would be devastated by what your parents did to you," she said, explaining further how it's a primary building block for children to feel secure in their attachment to where they are and who is caring for them. As a young child, you need to feel that no matter who you are, or what you do, your parents will figure out a way to work things out with you. My parents did no such thing. To them, I was a bother, a problem.

Those were the potentially healing messages that Diana would try to convey to me. She understood that as a therapist, sometimes you need to be able to shine the light on a path of understanding, acceptance, healing, and change, even when your client can't yet see that path.

And I was definitely not seeing it. Even if at least some of what Diana was saying was true, that still didn't explain why I was a complete failure at normal living now. Why couldn't I stick with school? Why couldn't I hold a job? Why couldn't I make my relationship work, when I so badly wanted and needed to have love in my life?

Unspoken sorrow, much regret. Hate her. Love her. I seethe with pain, even if she doesn't know it. I wish I could release her, let her go from my heart. I just melt and the tears flow and the pain sets my soul on fire.

Those were the words tumbling onto the page of my journal about the ending of my relationship with Ann, and the end of having a child to care for. My head was spinning with other questions: Why couldn't I get out of bed in the morning? Why did I not feel like eating anything except baloney sandwiches and soda? And why, when I was alone in my tiny apartment, was I usually engulfed in dark thoughts about my life and what I should do about it?

Much of Diana's day-to-day work with me was simply to monitor my behavior for serious suicidal thoughts. When we both agreed that my emotional state had reached a possible crisis point, she would guide me into a hospital. And she would be right there to watch over my treatment until all parties had determined that the crisis had passed and I could slide back into my home of solitude, where the same dark clouds would soon show up on the pages of my journal.

Everyone thinks I'm crazy, crazy, crazy. They'll be better off without me. I can't even seem to tell my mother how much she hurt me. I love her, it doesn't make sense really. I keep feeling like I'm the person who fails, and nobody wants to be around me...

Sometimes my words didn't just capture a melancholy moment. As the dark days piled on, one after another, they often spelled out the only way out I could imagine.

Death is safe
and I never feel safe.
Death is peaceful,
and I want peace.
Time drags by,
everything so slow.
I cry and cry,
I'm not sure why.
Why am I still so sick
when I have tried so hard?
Wouldn't God forgive me
for killing myself?

Diana was aware that I would have these kinds of suicidal thoughts from time to time. More than once she heard me proclaim, "This world's a terrible place." That's why she was closely watching and listening each time I got myself on the bus and rode to keep our appointments, and why she was quick to intervene when danger seemed real. Often, she would give me the reality test: did I have a plan to kill myself? I told her no, it was just an idea, the trail of where my mind would lead on those dreary days and nights. In fact, I was honest with Diana about almost everything that was happening to me...until I wasn't honest anymore.

Here's what happened. One day when I was explaining how the idea of death sometimes seemed like a relief to me, and that people suffering mental pain should be allowed to kill themselves just like those suffering physical pain from something like cancer, she had said something like, "I can understand your pain." Now today, I am quite sure that in the next few moments Diana went on to shed light on the bigger picture of my experience, and that she offered a lot of other life-affirming, therapeutically appropriate words. Only in my desperate state, all I heard was "I understand" which in my troubled state I translated into "I understand that you need to kill yourself, and it's okay if you do it."

I warmed up to the actual plan slowly.

Here's how I want to die. I want to be warm. I want to be held, told that I'm okay. I want to listen to Janis Joplin's Greatest Hits. *I want to overdose on pills, but I will eat ice cream so it doesn't hurt my stomach.*

Soon I was taking more concrete action steps. I made out a will, making it clear that a certain stuffed animal and two pieces of jewelry would go to Sarah. I also wrote her a letter, telling her how much I loved her, along with letters to my best friend Tim, the one who had AIDS, and to my friend Valerie, and separate letters to my foster mom and dad. I sold my car, my only real asset, and I packed up all the rest of my belongings in the apartment and labeled them with instructions for where to donate them. I called the power company and informed them of the exact date to switch off power in my apartment. I went to the library to research suicide and concluded that my best route would be to take a bunch of my antidepressants, along with an enormous quantity of Benadryl.

Oh, I had a plan all right, but nobody was going to know about it until it was mission accomplished. On the day I had circled, I went to the grocery store and plucked several boxes of Benadryl off the shelves. I was confident that if I took enough, I would go to sleep and never wake up. When I reached the checkout counter and noted the perplexed look the woman was giving me, I was quick with my cover story: "I work at a group home, you see, and we've got to stock up for allergy season." She rang up the Benadryl, along with my ice cream.

I arranged the mounds and mounds of pills on my second-hand dining table, with my personal letters that I had written close at hand. I started swallowing a bunch of pills at a time, with my ice cream chasers, and I was doing just fine until I had an overwhelming thought: I don't want to die alone. It was about midnight by then, so I decided that I would call the county mental health center crisis hotline, a service I had accessed a few other times. Recognizing that I should not call from my home phone because they could find out who I was, I walked through our parking lot, crossed the street and the railroad tracks, and headed toward the pay phone outside the 7-Eleven where I bought my baloney and bread. I put the coins in the slot.

"Hi. Well, I was going to kill myself but I didn't want to die alone, you know, and I've got every right to do it because people should be able to, like, euthanize themselves when they're in mental pain, and I've been in a lot of pain and I've tried to get out, tried and tried and, well, I just had to tell somebody. Goodbye."

I didn't let the woman manning the hotline get in a word in response, and I was careful not to hang on the phone long enough for her to try to trace the call. I felt bad for her, too. That must not have been an easy phone call to receive. But I was on a mission...

Despite feeling woozy, I made it back to my apartment, rearranged some of the packed boxes and sat myself back down at the table. I looked at the remaining pile of pills, took a breath and got back to work. Somewhere along the line, I managed to stagger to my bed and settle in for the longest sleep I had ever had...

"Kris! Kris! Kris, wake up!!" I could hear voices yelling from the side of my bed. *No, no, no one's supposed to come here. That's not part of my plan. You need to leave right now!* I couldn't speak my protests out loud, however, and a few minutes later in my dreamy fog I was certain that I was flying in an airplane when in reality I was riding in an ambulance. Then I slipped back into the fog and didn't come out until I heard more yelling.

"She's arresting!" someone shouted, and they were all over me with their equipment, doing their compressions and other frantic procedures. *This is it. I'm dying now. I'm going, going, and they won't be able to get me back*. I imagined someone speaking to me, softly: "We're going to let you die now."

Only that's not what happened, because the next thing I knew I was in some kind of restraints, like what I remembered from the psychiatric hospitals, and they were moving me from the ER into Intensive Care. I was connected to a whole slew of heart monitors and other wires and devices, and I heard voices of people all around. I knew they were talking about me, and I was convinced that they were conspiring to do something terrible to me. I think the first words I babbled were something like, "You can't, don't hurt me, I know you're all talking about how you're going to hurt me."

"That's just the effect of the medication, Sweetheart," a nurse said as she leaned in close to me. "Nobody's talking about you in any bad way. We're not going to do anything to hurt you. You'll feel better soon."

I sighed. In that moment, I knew that my plan had failed. I was going to live.

When my condition had stabilized enough to leave Intensive Care, the plan was to move me to the psychiatric unit. I was awake when the psychiatrist came to assess me. He informed me that I had been discovered in my apartment at about 9 the morning after I had consumed all those pills, which meant I had been overdosing about nine hours before the first responders got to me. One more hour, he said, and it would definitely have been too late. He also let me know that my heart had stopped on the ER table.

"You're a very lucky young woman," he said.

Lucky, huh? I was supposed to die! I managed to ask him how they found me. I was furious.

"Oh, that was your therapist, Diana," he said. "She called 911 and told them they needed to get to you right away. You called her from your bed in your apartment. Guess you woke yourself up just in time."

I sat upright in bed. *I called Diana? What is this guy talking about? I never called Diana. I only made that one call to the crisis hotline, but that was way back at midnight, not 9 a.m., and I didn't stay on long enough for them to find me.*

I wanted to argue with him, to make him understand that I did not call for help, that I really had wanted to kill myself. Otherwise they would think that this was not a serious suicide attempt and they would not understand that I really did not want anyone coming to my apartment until I was...

I let my body slump back down on the hospital bed.

So how did Diana know?

12

In the Womb, Part II

My friend Tonya was surveying my apartment after picking me up from the psychiatric ward. The electricity had been shut off, just as I had ordered. There was no dial tone on my phone—that service had been stopped, too. She didn't see the letters I had left behind that night because the police had picked them up and taken them away as evidence. Glancing around in the semi-darkness, Tonya noted all the carefully packed and marked boxes, and the empty cabinets and shelves.

"Wow, you were really ready to go," she said.

"Yes, I was, by God," I said with a slight chuckle. *The question now is whether I'm ready for what's next.*

I walked slowly toward the open bedroom and glanced inside. Noticing the dried vomit on the bed, I turned away. *I could have choked to death...* I grabbed a few belongings and signaled Tonya that it was time for us to get out. She took me to a restaurant, where I picked at my food and stared across the dining area.

"You should call your therapist," said Tonya. "Let her know you're out of the hospital."

Diana? Yes, it was time to talk with Diana. When I called the county mental health center, they confirmed that an appointment for me to see her had already been scheduled for the next day. I was told that at the hospital but had already forgotten.

"Diana is not available to talk right now, but I'm sure she would want to know that you called," the receptionist said. "Can you hang on a few minutes?"

"Well, I'm at a pay phone at a restaurant," I said. "But I'll try."

So, I waited and waited, worrying about what Diana would say to me. Would she be angry that I tried to kill myself? Then again, she had said that she understood that I needed to end my life. Didn't she? It must have been 15 minutes later when I heard her voice come on the line.

"Kris, I'm so glad you're alive!" she said. "And Kris, life does matter. Life…does…matter. Now I'm going to see you tomorrow at 10 a.m., but right now I want you to get out some paper and take down my home phone number. Tonight, if you feel that you need to talk to me at any time, for any reason, I want you to call me."

Wow, Diana really cares about me, I thought. Tonya let me stay with her that night, and the next morning I showed up early for my therapy appointment. As soon as we sat down together, I asked Diana about telling me in our last session that she thought it was okay for me to kill myself.

"No, I never thought that would be okay," Diana said calmly. "I said that I understood your pain."

She filled me in on what else she had told me that day, after I had stopped listening, and reminded me of all the work we had done together for several months to make sure that I was safe.

"I know. I guess I just finally decided that I needed to die," I mumbled. "And I did such good planning. They told me that one more hour in my bedroom and I would have been gone. But then you called 911 and… Diana, did I call you that morning? I can't believe I would have done that, but that's what the psychiatrist at the hospital told me."

"No, you didn't call me," she explained, and then she grinned. "I'll tell you what happened."

Diana had come to work early that morning after I had swallowed all those antidepressants and Benadryl. She had to cover for a co-worker who had called in sick. One of that co-worker's tasks that morning would have been to conduct a debrief meeting with the crisis hotline volunteers, to discover if any calls that had come in during the night needed follow-up. Diana sat down with the crisis hotline volunteer who had taken my midnight call from the 7-Eleven and listened to her report: "She just kept saying she didn't want to die alone. Oh, and that she thought she should have the right to kill herself, like someone suffering with terminal cancer."

Those words told Diana everything she needed to know. She bolted out of the conference room and rushed to her desk. Finding my phone number on her files, she quickly dialed my apartment. She let the phone ring ten times, maybe more, and then hung up and called 911. After urgently explaining the situation, she urged the police to conduct an immediate welfare check at my apartment. And that's how I was saved.

"I had never covered that debrief meeting before," Diana said. "And if it was anyone else listening to that report from the hotline, they would not have known it was you. It was just a coincidence that I was there, and that I made that call."

A coincidence? Hmmmm. We both sat in silence for a few moments.

"I have to clean up my apartment," I said finally. "And I've got to call to get the power turned back on, and the phone and all that."

"No, you can't live alone," Diana responded. "That would be too much for you right now."

"Well, I'm not going back into some group home, and I sure don't want to go to the state hospital or any other place in that whole system because—"

"You're going to move in with your parents," Diana interjected.

"What? They don't even know what happened," I said.

"Well, actually, they do," Diana said, and she reminded me how I had once signed a release allowing her to talk with Bev and Gary if needed at some point during the course of my therapy. "We've already talked, and we are all in agreement that the best thing for you right now is to stay with them for a while."

I wanted to protest, to spout off about how unfair it was that this had been decided behind my back, and to make another loud stand about how I was just going to go on living on my own. Instead, I took a breath and just looked at Diana. She looked back at me. And in that quiet moment, I realized that I didn't know what was best for me. I was in too much pain. I would just have to let go and let someone else make decisions for me. And of all the people I knew in the world, Diana was the one I trusted most.

"Okay," I said with a slight nod.

"Good! When you go home after our session today, your parents are going to be there waiting for you. They'll help you pack up your things so you can move out of your apartment and move in with them."

I stifled a chuckle. I had already done all that packing up before I was carted off to the emergency room. I was going to be leaving that apartment, one way or another.

When I headed home, I found Bev and my dad waiting for me in the parking lot.

"There you are!" Bev said in her usual cheerful voice. She didn't say anything about my unsuccessful attempt to kill myself. She was all business, taking charge of the task at hand: pick out the few things I would need to live in her house and get the rest of my stuff in storage. Gary had already attached a U-Haul trailer to their car.

The first thing that caught my eye when I walked into their home, that same house I had lived in for nine months as a teenager, was the yellow wallpaper with the Asian design in the living room. I had loved that wallpaper when I was there. It was so pretty. Looking around further, I saw that not much else had changed in the 11 years since I had stormed out, knocking all the glass out of the garage windows along the way. Of course, only the two younger kids, Erik and Julie, were still around. Julie was right around the same age I was when Bev took me in that first time, and Erik had just entered the teen years. Bev told me I could stay in the same room, the converted sewing room, where I had lived when I was 15. She told me to bring up my bag of clothes and come right back downstairs so we could talk.

What are they going to expect of me? I thought. *I'm not a kid anymore, I'm 26 years old. But I'm so tired. Bev is so active in church and social causes and all that. I'm not sure I can keep up with what she may want from me.*

"So, here's what we've decided," she said when we sat down together. "First, you can stay here as long as you need to. Second, we want you to continue to see Diana regularly. Last thing, we want you to show up here for dinner every night. That's the sum total of what we expect right now. Kris, you just need to rest."

Wow, Bev still really knows me! She hit it exactly right. And here she is, offering to help me now, after all this time, after what just happened... I was just so tired.

And that's the foundation that, over time, would help me rebuild my life. Bev and Diana formed two pillars on either side of me, ready and waiting to hold me up when I tilted one way or another, or came close to crumbling down in a heap.

I remember one moment, about two months after Bev took me in, when we were sitting together on the sofa in the family room.

"Welcome to the world," she said with a glimmer in her eye. "You deserve to be alive."

I liked those words so much that I tried them on for myself. For several mornings in a row, I would wake up and say to myself, "Welcome to the world. You deserve to be alive." At that point, I can't say that I one hundred percent believed that, but it was something at least worth considering.

I adhered to Bev's simple expectations. Not only did I show up for dinner, I also began to spend more time hanging around the two teenagers in the house. Julie was interested in how I reached the point of suicide and what I was doing to try to recover, and I confided in her like a friend. She heard everything, even the part about my off-and-on work as a prostitute. Between the moments of sharing my darkness, I also could allow in a little more light. When the three of us watched *Saturday Night Live* together, I even laughed at some of the jokes.

As Bev and I spent more and more time talking, it wasn't always just about me. Back when I was a wild and unruly teenager, I didn't have much interest in hearing much about her life. Now I was more curious. I learned she had suffered her own childhood trauma while she was growing up in Colorado. Bev got out as soon as she could, married her first husband and had three kids with him, including Kathy, then divorced and eventually met my dad. Gary was an engineer in New Mexico at the time, and as well as having Julie and Erik, together, they took in the two foster children I had heard about. Apparently those two girls eventually wound up back with their own families.

Seeing Bev as a full human being, not just the woman who rescued me from a freezing cold car as a teenager, gave me even more respect for her. This time around, I also could see more clearly how much time and effort she devoted to helping other people and the world. She was still active in her Unitarian Church, the Rotary, the local Food Bank and many other causes. She liked to dress up, and could really turn on the glitz and glamour when she wanted to, but she was equally at home going out with her family in their little tent camper. She was a warm and real person, and although she preferred to approach others in her kind and loving manner, she was no pushover. She could be strong as hell when the situation called for it. I could attest to that.

And now I was the fortunate recipient of all that strength, love, caring and compassion that poured from this short woman with the red hair. She accepted me for who I was, with all my history, and she looked for every possible opportunity to remind me that I had value. She understood my vulnerability, but she also recognized my strength. In doing so, she was beginning to spark a growing determination in me.

Cray Cray

The whole Conaway family was cheering me on. They would tell me how proud they were of me for sticking with my therapy, for trying to turn the corner. Gary was much quieter around the house, but we did share one moment that spoke volumes about how he felt about me. I was still a smoker then, and since there was a firm family rule of no smoking in the house, I would go out to the front stoop when I needed to light up. One day my dad came out and sat right down beside me. Our shoulders were lightly touching, and I was struck by how unusual this was because no one in the family would come into my space when I held a cigarette in my hand. I waited for Gary to decide when to break the silence.

"I can't say that I totally understand how things have been for you in your life," he said. "I don't have the personal experience to relate. But what I do know is that you've got a spark in you that we almost lost. But now that spark is coming back. I can see it."

I snuffed out my cigarette and allowed Gary's words to echo in my mind. And he wasn't done.

"You know," he said, "if there's one thing I know about you, it's that you are a fighter. Yep, you're a fighter all right and…and you're going to make it."

Then he put his arm around me and gave me a sideways hug. I rested my head on his shoulders and just leaned into him, just as I was leaning into the whole experience of being held, and loved, by this family and this environment. I felt entirely safe in their embrace. I now knew that they weren't going to throw me out of the house, and there was no way I was going to do anything to make them boot me out the door. I was no longer the wounded animal, constantly ready to lash out whenever she perceived potential danger. "You can stay for as long as you need to," Bev had said, and she had meant it. They all did.

Beyond just showing up for dinner, I also began to come down early and watch Bev cook. As I observed her prepare those simple chicken dishes and casseroles, with plenty of salads and vegetables, I appreciated just how important it was for her to provide nurturing food for her family.

Over time, I even began to help her cook, and I reached the point of being able to solo on a few meals. "Culinary therapy," Bev called it with a gentle laugh. I also pitched in with the dishes. I understood that this family, my family, was giving a lot to me and I wanted to give something back to them. I was bonding with them all in ways that throughout my childhood, adolescence and early adulthood I had never bonded with anyone. In psychology, they call it a corrected healing relationship.

Bev also encouraged me to start thinking outside of myself, to see the bigger world and how I could contribute to it. She got me involved in some of her political causes, and I gravitated to some of my own. I actively stood up against the first Gulf War and marched for gay rights. Even when Bev and I disagreed, we could talk about our opinions and really listen to one another. In the safety of her home, for the second time in my life, it was like my whole lens of life just kept expanding.

In therapy, Diana reinforced the same message.

"You can have more in your life," she would say. "You can be anything you want to be."

Of course, we had more work to do on healing my past. Diana dug in to help me explore why I had reached the point where I felt like such a failure that I would be better off dead. I allowed remnants of the old pain to bubble up, and slowly began to let more of it go. All along, she kept validating my experience, reminding me again and again that I had a right to feel what I was feeling, no matter how yucky it might look or sound.

At some point, she moved our sessions out of the small consultation room where we had always met into some kind of group room about three times the size. Instead of just sitting and talking about my old wounds, I would get up and walk around the large space. While expressing my feelings and recounting my memories orally, I also began to shake my arms around and dart one way and then another. With so much that still needed to come out now, I had to physically move it, so I could totally release it. I would not have known the term for it then, but today I can see that Diana and I had added somatic work to my healing.

I also recognize that, all along, Diana was helping to facilitate my positive attachment with her. She began to share more about her own personal life when appropriate. She had three daughters and would tell me when one of them was visiting from Seattle or San Francisco, and she described how much she loved her granddaughter. I could better appreciate that my therapist was a real person, with a life of her own, not just a provider of mental health services. I also learned that she had not even earned a Master's degree in her field. I didn't care. Diana was a healer, and she was totally devoted to my healing. That's all that mattered.

Both before my suicide attempt, and now in the aftermath of my near-death experience, she was steadfast in her commitment to keep shining a light on my possible future. For much longer than I would have liked, I couldn't see the world of possibility that was opening up in front of me. Diana never gave up on me, never got discouraged.

And then, a few months after I tried to kill myself, the switch just flipped. I could finally see the light on the path ahead for myself. With Diana's wise and deeply caring guidance, and Bev's loving nurturance and support, I finally got it. Life did matter. I was more than my past, no matter how painful and traumatic it had been. Perhaps I just got sick and tired of being sick and tired, pissed off about the state of my life and determined to rebel against what had been done to me and what I had been deprived of for so long.

Instead of all that old hopeless and foreboding self-talk in my suicide journal, the messages reverberating all around me now had a totally different tone:

I'll be damned if I'm going to let my history be in charge of my future.

I'm never going to be locked up again!

I'm dropping my identity as a psychiatric patient right now. That's not who I am. I deserve more than that.

The dramatic change totally shifted the focus of my therapy sessions. Suddenly, it felt as if there was nothing more I had to say about what had happened during my childhood and adolescence, and no more processing about this recent and near-tragic phase of struggle and heartache. Diana had allowed and encouraged me to talk and talk and talk about all of that, and now the bucket was empty. I had dumped it all out. I was opening the door to the outside world, rubbing my eyes and taking in everything in my sights in a whole new light.

I let go of all the old questions: what happened to me, how was I hurt, how did that impact me, how did the identity of a crazy person tie me down? Now I began to bring in new questions: What did I want in life? Who did I want to be? What really mattered to me? What were the possibilities that lay ahead?

Every day that I showed up to meet with Diana, I was full of new energy and anticipation. While walking toward her office for one of our meetings, I had the physical sensation of light moving through my body, like a beam of light was just coming right out of me. I was just beginning to tune into that experience when I crossed a man on the sidewalk.

"Miss, oh Miss," he called out as we passed. When I turned around he said, "I just want to tell you that you are beautiful, and that you have this amazing light around you."

"Thank you," was all I could think of to say in response.

"Thank *you*," he added, and then to make clear that he had no other agenda, he just kept walking away.

That was certainly a new experience! When I told Diana all about it in our session that day, she just smiled. "Expect many more new experiences like that," she said.

Diana knew when to cheer me on, and when to hand me a challenge. I had been mentioning off and on that I should get serious about school again, and that if I were really going to position myself for a college degree, I would first need to get my high school GED. She was aware that so far, that had only been talk.

"So, I guess we should just accept that you're probably not going to have further education as part of your future, like you said you would have," she said one day. "Guess that whole GED thing is just off the table now. Let's be intentional about that. You know, set it aside as not so important to you anymore so we can—"

"What do you mean it's not important to me?" I sputtered. "Oh, I see. You think I'm not smart enough to get a GED, right?

"I'm not saying that," Diana countered. "I think you are smart enough to do it. I just think maybe you're just—"

"Okay, we'll just see about that," I said, as the session came to a close. After leaving Diana's office, I marched right down to community college and asked for directions to the department that handled the GED program.

"I want to take the GED test…right now," I said when I got there.

"You can't. You have to take the prep classes first and see how you would test. There are five tests you have to pass to earn your GED, you know," I was told.

"I don't care," I demanded. "I want to take all five tests now. If I don't pass one or two, then I'll take those stupid classes."

"Well, all right then. Come back tomorrow and we can set up the five tests for you."

When I sat down to tackle the GED tests the next day, I was still thinking: *Diana thinks I'm stupid. I'll show her.* And I passed all five tests. Piece of cake.

"So, here's that GED," I announced to Diana as I plunked down the certificate at the start of our next session.

Diana looked over the paper, nodded her head, and then looked up at me.

"Okay, then," she said with a serious expression. "So where do you go from here?"

Well, for starters it was time to start finding ways to help other people, something I had begun to do when I was younger but always on what seemed like an interim basis. I began with volunteer work, taking slots on a crisis line for women dealing with domestic violence. Then

I volunteered with the VISTA program, assisting homeless youths. I certainly knew something about that life! I was sleeping better, feeling stronger and enjoying these opportunities to be productive.

At home, my bonding and attachment to Bev and my family just kept growing. Somewhere along the line, we talked about shifting our relationship to an actual adoption. As it turned out, we didn't take that step. Instead we just came to an understanding that I was adopted in my heart. I didn't need the legal part.

Bev also stepped in to assist me on another front, helping me navigate the terrain that eventually opened the door for me to start seeing Sarah. Spending time with this wonderful child again, I was grateful to find that she and I still shared a deep mutual connection. That was one more important way for me to fully re-enter the world.

Then it was time for me to get my own place to live. When I found an affordable apartment, I told Bev that I would be moving out. It was February, and I noted to myself that I had moved in while in my shell-shocked state the previous May. That meant it had been exactly nine months since Bev had taken me in soon after I had tried to end my life. Now she had been instrumental in my getting that life back. *Nine months, same as the first time,* I thought. This was not a dramatic parting, though, nothing like my big production with my dad as a teenager. This time it was very clear that Bev and my foster family would remain very much in my life.

I began to take classes at community college again, with a new sense of direction. Taking subjects such as sociology and psychology enabled me to follow my curiosity, succeed in something I had natural ability in and position myself for a solid potential profession.

"I want to be a therapist," I told Diana one day.

"Yes," she said after a long pause. "And I have no doubt that you will have much to offer in that work."

I decided that to seriously pursue this career track, I would need to do it somewhere other than Portland. I'm not sure why this was true, but somehow I just had an intuitive sense that I needed to step out of the shadows of the area where I had suffered so much in order to help alleviate the suffering of others. I had begun to learn to listen to my intuition, to pay attention to signs for what to do or where to go.

Once I had narrowed my choices for my new home to Seattle and San Francisco, I cut an index card in half and wrote down one city on one half and the other city on the other half and stuck both cards under my pillow. "When I wake up in the morning, whichever card I reach for first will be the place I will go," I told myself.

Seattle. Diana was totally supportive of my choice, although this would mean the end of our active therapist-client relationship. Before our work was complete, I focused a little more time reflecting on my near-suicide, to explore what else I might learn from my experience that could help me in going forward. I thought again about that moment when my heart stopped in the emergency room and the frantic nurses and doctors scrambled to reverse a course that appeared destined for me to go. With Diana's guidance, I concluded that maybe I really did die that day. That is, a *part* of me was dying—the wounded part, the hopeless part, the part that had cemented the identity of a mental patient deep inside. Oh, I'll always have that part with me, but not in the way of feeling persecuted, of being the victim. If I was "dying" in some way, it was dying to a new way of life.

I also considered again how Diana had come to be in the position of hearing about my crisis intervention call and to leap into action, just in time. Was that really just a coincidence? No, I didn't think so anymore. I believed that those circumstances all came together the way they did because Diana was so connected to me. I could not have explained it then, and I'm not sure I can even explain it fully today, but I think somehow that Diana was supposed to be there that morning when she was filling in for that co-worker and heard the crisis volunteer describe my call on the hotline. Yes, somehow or other, everything happened just the way it was supposed to happen…

When I told Bev about my plan to leave the Portland area, she was a bit resistant at first.

"Do you really need to leave to pursue your profession?" she said, but after listening to me try to explain what I couldn't fully explain to myself, she shifted gears.

"Then I guess the question to ask is, will you regret it if you didn't go up there to see if it's the right place for you?" she said.

"I think I would regret it," I said.

"Then you need to go."

To demonstrate her support, she made me an offer. By that point, I had saved some money from work at a residential treatment center and invested $5,000 in a car. Bev at that time, was driving the family's second car, an old Honda.

"Here's what we'll do," she said. "You can have my Honda for $500. You can keep it down here for when you come to visit, or when you come back to Portland to live after you get your degree. I'll pay you the $5,000 you paid for your car, so you can have some cash for rent and everything else you'll need."

I agreed to my mom's generous offer and, before long, it was time to punch my one-way train ticket to Seattle and hug my family goodbye. As tears spilled out, it occurred to me that in stepping out of Bev's orbit, I was leaving the womb for the second time in my adolescent and adult life. Only this time, I was totally ready to go.

13

Graduation Day

We were all lined up in our graduation gowns, preparing to walk down the aisle to receive our diplomas from the Leadership Institute of Seattle in conjunction with Bastyr University. I had to cut closer to the front of the line for a moment, just so I could get a better look at the people waiting to watch us from the pews of the downtown church hosting our event. I scanned to the left, to the right and to the center. At last I spotted her red hair. Bev!

My mom and Dad had come up from Portland to see me graduate. Looking further at where she and Gary were sitting, I noticed several friends from back home that had also made the drive for my big day. Four, five, six...there were ten people all in one row who had traveled to celebrate with me. Every one of them knew what it had taken for me to get from where I had been to where I was now, earning a college degree and moving ever closer to making my dream of becoming a therapist a reality. They all had the biggest smiles on their faces, and I was beaming back at them.

Our graduation ceremony was held in the church because our college was housed in a former Buddhist monastery, and this facility better accommodated our needs. After we were awarded our diplomas, the graduation festivities were scheduled to progress to a cruise on Puget Sound.

"Oh, baby, you did it!" Bev cried out as we hugged. She and Gary and all the others from my personal rooting section were going along with me on the early dinner cruise. My parents had paid the $80 for my ticket, a welcome gesture since the ongoing effort to scrounge up the money to pay for my education had left me broke. My friend Karen from school had taken me to Macy's and bought me a dress suitable to wear on the celebratory outing. It was my first experience of shopping for myself in a real downtown department store.

It was quite the shindig: cloth napkins, lobster, local salmon, fancy desserts, plenty of wine. I danced, hugged, got caught up with old friends, and I stopped bouncing around long enough to receive my presents. Mom gave me a beautiful set of diamond earrings, as well as a check for $1,000. "I have just one requirement," she explained, and I immediately flashed to those simple expectations she had laid out for me when I came to live with her soon after trying to end my life. "I want this money to go toward purchasing your own computer."

As Bev knew, I had been getting by with library computers when needed during those days in the '90s, just before all our lives were taken over by electronics. A new computer back then cost close to $2,000, so this gift would make a huge down payment for my future. My plan was to go on to grad school, although I would likely need a year off to line up the finances and rev up my academic engines again. Obtaining a college degree had been a steep climb for the girl who had dropped out of school in ninth grade, but I never worried about sliding back down the hill. I had come much too far to fail.

After the cruise wrapped up just after sunset, I hosted a graduation party for friends in a meeting space in the Seattle Garden Club. I danced and danced, and found room to eat some more because my friends had brought food to the party. I never wanted the night to end. I'm a college graduate! I kept thinking. How did I ever get here?

The truth was that I certainly did not do it alone. Upon first arriving

Cray Cray

in Seattle, I had to stay in a hostel until I found a place to live and a job to support myself while obtaining more community college credits before I could transfer to a four-year college. I wound up securing another position working with the young homeless population. During my previous experience with VISTA in Portland, I was entrusted with serving as a case manager for residents between the ages of 17 and 21. I could personally relate to the challenges and issues these young people were grappling with in our residential program that taught independent living skills. One teenage girl especially caught my eye. Our backgrounds were different, but she was a fighter, a real spitfire like me. She needed that fighting spirit to have survived years of drug use and resulting liver damage. She was also sensitive, and vulnerable, and I could relate to that, too. It was rewarding to stand with her as she began to find the strength to rebuild her life.

When I began to look for a four-year college, I focused my initial attention on Antioch University Seattle. Before I took the final steps to enroll there, a co-worker who was on course to receive a Master's degree recommended the Leadership Institute. I knew nothing about the institute or Bastyr then, but I liked what he said and agreed to check it out. From my initial interview, it seemed like all the planets had aligned for me to attend this exciting program geared for adult students. In fact, when I entered while still in my 20s, I was the youngest student in my group. Most of them were over 35, and many had a proven track record of success in one career and maybe a family of their own. I was the "baby" of the class, but after being the youngest in many "unusual" environments from my pre-teen years on, I knew something about making my way around the older crowd.

I made many new friends, but none were more important or influential than the woman who I met over a shared connection with a certain fast-food restaurant. Liz was eating her lunch in the staff room of the center where I worked to support the young homeless population that day I walked in and found her. I smiled when I saw the familiar hamburger and fries.

"I see you like Burger King," I said.

"Yep, got to have my BK burger and fries to keep me going," she said with a grin.

"Well, you know, I used to work at Burger King near Portland," I said. "I remember wearing that silly uniform when I was 15 years old. But I needed the job because I was living on my own."

"Wow," she said, "how did you come to be on your own when you were so young?"

"Oh," I responded with a grin, "that's a long story."

And so I told her, not all at once, but piece by piece when we had time to talk. I didn't leave any important piece out, which was unusual for me in this new city where people did not know my history. When others asked about my family, I would usually only refer to Bev and the rest of the Conaways. I might mention that I was "adopted" or that I was a foster child, but I didn't go into the part about watching my birth mother try to kill herself when I was four, or getting thrown out of schools for fighting students and teachers, or being raised in psychiatric hospitals, or making money to live on my own via the sex-for-survival plan. While these others who I met at work, in college or anywhere else, were getting the condensed version of Kristy's roots, Liz was being given a view of the full picture.

The striking thing was, her own picture looked somewhat like mine. She had run away from home at a young age herself, managing to get out of her home state on a Greyhound bus before her parents tracked her down and she ended up in a hospital. Liz's experience was in a general hospital ward, rather than a psychiatric facility, but she still had rigid rules and tough-minded staff to navigate. Once when she was ordered not to leave her room until notified otherwise, she stuck her big toe outside her door into the hallway, just to see what would happen. We shared more than a few laughs over bizarre episodes of being treated as a young person with psychological issues, but we also shared the pain we had suffered and the battle to endure and eventually rise above it. Liz and I soon became thick as thieves. This was the kind of friendship I had been longing for, a peer who I could relate to with the same kind of openness and depth I shared with Bev and Diana back home. It was one of the greatest gifts I received in my entire experience of living in Seattle.

When our friendship first began to take root, Liz was pursuing her Master's in Social Work from the University of Washington. She had exceptional writing skills, and that was one area in which we had no commonality. I had never taken a real writing class, and after I had enrolled at Bastyr, I was suddenly expected to write and write and write. At times, I wondered if the writing requirements might derail my college career, but Liz was having none of that kind of thinking. "You can do this," she would tell me over and over again, and she offered the hands-on guidance to support my efforts. I don't know whether I would have ever made it without her.

Liz also helped me weather a storm that swirled up just before the final year of my undergraduate program. I was called in by school administration and informed that, due to a mix-up or oversight related to my transcripts before I enrolled, I was actually dozens of credits short of graduation. That meant that not only would I have to take a full course load during my senior year, but also that I would have to enroll in wall-to-wall courses at community college to make up the difference in credits. All while still working to pay for my living expenses.

"You can do anything you want to do in your life," Diana had told me. So, with Liz standing beside me every step of the way, I figured out how to finish my college education. Don Warner and Katherine Johnson, my staunch allies in our school administration, educated me about CLEP (College Level Examination Program) and how you can earn needed college credits for what you already know. So, I "CLEPPED" out of several credits and managed to squeeze in just enough classroom time to fill in the gaps at community college so I could still graduate with my class.

I considered a couple of graduate programs in California but eventually decided that I liked the people and the teachings at the Leadership Institute so much it just made sense to stay right there to pursue my

Master's. During my gap year between my undergrad and graduate studies, I attended classes at the University of Washington and completed a certification program in the treatment of long-term, chronic mental illness.

This new commitment in my education delivered two more daunting challenges. Academically, I had to complete what they called the culmination project, which required research at the level of a dissertation. I enjoyed doing the research component for my project, in which I examined the impact of institutionalization on women who were treated in one or more psychiatric facilities as girls. I certainly knew the subject, but the writing requirement was a major challenge. Liz almost literally sat at my keyboard with me to help pull me along.

"Just start talking your ideas and I'll write them down," she instructed. Then she led me into reading over and assessing my dictated notes, looking for ideas and themes to explore. She began tearing off sheets of paper with these notes and hanging them up for us to brainstorm together. Within days, all the walls of my apartment were filled with scribbled notes. Gradually, the notes were translated into my writing, with Liz tirelessly contributing to the project with her editing and advising. "You can do it," she kept saying, although the truth was that "we" could do it.

Liz was my anchor in the push to complete the required academic work for my Master's, and for that I will always be grateful to her. But even before I could begin that final push, I began desperately seeking an anchor on the financial side. I continued my work at or near full-time through my first year in the program while living with my girlfriend at the time. The tuition was steep, and money was tight. My diet mostly consisted of beans and rice, tortillas with cream cheese and pepper jam, and popcorn with Brewer's yeast. I was borrowing money at a rate that was beginning to drag me down. I had been living on a wing and a prayer, but if I were going to make it to this new finish line, something or someone was going to have to show up to give me a boost.

And that's exactly what happened. One day, Dan Lahey, one of my faculty supporters, pulled me aside and told me about a group that he served as a volunteer. It was called Washington Women in Need (WWIN). "They provide educational grants to women just like you," he explained. "I know you'd be a great candidate. Why don't you apply?" At first, I couldn't grasp the idea that these awards were not loans, which by that point I knew a whole lot about, but actual never-pay-it-back scholarships. Once I understood that, I jumped on it immediately.

As I approached this organization, I fully expected to have to prove my need via some 15-page document, backed by detailed financial statements and hours of intense and grueling interviews in front of some big committee. Boy, was I wrong. To apply, I merely had to write a one-page essay explaining in my own way why I needed financial support, how I would use the educational grant, and what my goals were in going forward with my education and my life. That was one writing assignment that I didn't have to sweat!

I sat down and quickly shaped the nutshell version of how I had survived my upbringing in the foster care system and institutional environments, and how I had been making it on my own since I was 15. I said that I was on the long stretch of a very long road, and how getting a nudge forward now would mean the world to me. Then I spoke of my strong desire to earn a graduate degree so I could become a professional therapist, where I would use what I learned from getting through my rough background to help others and maybe even the world.

The "interview" phase of the application process consisted of meeting with one representative of the organization for less than an hour. This woman simply read over my essay and asked me a couple of follow-up questions to gain more details about my career aspirations. She didn't ask for any tax forms. It was clear that in seeking this money, I didn't have to beg or grovel. I was treated with absolute respect.

Within days after my interview, I received a letter from Washington Women in Need. "We are pleased to inform you that you have been granted a full scholarship for the upcoming academic year..." *No way! That can't be. There has to be more to it than that,* I thought. I reread the letter, twice, and showed it to Liz before I could fully accept the reality that my entire tuition bill for my second and final year of grad school was being covered by this wonderful program. I wasn't even being required to report back to them at any point in the future, to verify that I had continued to pursue and eventually achieve the goals I had outlined in applying for the grant. I also was still eligible to receive the loan that I had already applied for, so I was able to use that money to live on. That meant that I could let go of my job working with the homeless, freeing up the critical time and energy to push through in school. This experience just affirmed for me again that in my new life, borne out of my healing after trying to kill myself, things just seemed to keep happening to propel me forward. Whatever I needed, and whenever I needed it, somehow seemed to emerge on my path.

I still considered both Bev and Diana as vital components of this magical spirit. Bev was there when I received my Master's degree, of course, even though she and Gary had divorced by then. We had maintained regular contact all along my educational track. I took the train down to Portland to visit her and other family and friends when I could, and she made the trek up to Seattle once. That visit was especially touching to me, because when I had lived with Bev after my suicide attempt, it never felt like it was just she and I. We did have private conversations, of course, but she had her husband and her family around, and all her other commitments. I valued her presence always but yearned for a time when it would be just the two of us. This visit was that opportunity.

I was living in a small, finished basement of an old house next to a junkyard at the time. When Bev stepped inside and looked around, she didn't flinch. She just sat right down on one end of the little futon that I used as a sofa. As I took my place on the other end, Bev brought her legs up on the sofa and crisscrossed them. She was sitting in the same way I almost always sat! We just sat and talked and laughed and talked some more, about things serious and not so serious. I thanked her for driving three and a half hours just to see me.

Bev took me to dinner, and I gave her my bed to sleep on while I slept on the futon sofa. The next morning, I asked her if she would go to my church with me. I had been attending regular services at the Church of Religious Science, which had become a vital part of my new spiritual journey. Bev was still committed to her Unitarian Church, but without hesitating for a moment, she agreed to come see my church.

The woman minister that day delivered an inspiring message—at least to me. In her talk, she suggested that if you believed that God was just one singular person or entity, your God may be too small. She emphasized that God looks different to different people, and that this is okay, and that God is in us and outside us, working through all of us, and that we are all connected. I wasn't sure how Bev was taking in this message, so when I watched her hold onto the collection plate being handed around and write a $500 check to tuck inside, I gasped. Bev was never flashy about spending money. Perhaps she was just making a generous contribution to my spiritual growth.

When we talked about the message after the service, however, Bev revealed that the minister's words had touched her personally. For years she had consistently regarded her community service and social justice work as her sole spiritual practice. The idea that there was any sort of God entity out there, watching over us and working through us, seemed like a fairy tale to her. But after enduring a recent health crisis, she had found herself re-evaluating her concept of God. The minister's message that morning gave her shifting ideas a sense of shape and meaning. She was grateful that I had brought her to listen.

During that visit, in which we also managed to have plenty of fun, one more seed had been planted to grow in our bond. My plan at that time was to return to Portland to live for a while after completing my Master's, and after this visit I was even more excited about the prospect of sharing more time with my mother during that transition.

Once, while I was visiting Bev in Portland while still pursuing my studies in Seattle, I decided to reach out to Diana. Like many former clients of therapists, I wanted to fill her in on my progress, to show her how far I had come. I also just missed her presence.

"Yes, I'd be happy to see you," Diana said when I called and asked if we could get together. "And since you're not my patient anymore, we don't need to meet in my office. Let's get together for coffee."

She was already there waiting for me when I approached Coffee People, Portland's local coffee house chain. She was sitting at an outside table with a little umbrella over it, with a cup of espresso in front of her. She was still wearing black, and her hair was now silver-grey. She had aged in the years since I left, but to me she was still a beautiful woman.

When she stood up to greet me, her hip caught the edge of the table, jarring her a bit. *That's the first misstep I have ever seen Diana make*, I thought with a grin. We hugged, and after I ordered my drink I told her all about Seattle: getting my undergrad degree, and the challenges I had to overcome along the way, my deepening bond with Bev, my continued work with young homeless people, my spiritual growth, and the wonderful gift I had received from Washington Women in Need. She just kept beaming at me in that proud parent way.

"So, what's new in your life?" I asked Diana, eager to show her that I didn't need to have all the attention focused on me and my life anymore. She explained that while she was still working in mental health, she had shifted from doing therapy to working for the State of Oregon. In her role, she served as investigator and advisor for cases where men and women in major distress had been placed on a 72-hour hold to determine if they needed to be committed to a psychiatric hospital. Once she assessed the case in front of her, she would make her recommendation to the court as to whether the person should be committed long term or whether she or he should be released, with a firm plan in place for extensive outpatient support.

As Diana explained it, she always kept her eye out for some way to provide needed help and support for people in the midst of some kind of psychiatric episode without being forced to enter the hospital system. She certainly knew the potential wounds that women and men of any age can suffer from being placed in an institutional setting. As I listened to Diana explain what she did, I couldn't help thinking how I wish she had been around in that role when my case would come up in the courts during my childhood. Maybe she could have found a different way for my problems to be treated...

"There's another reason I wanted to see you," I said after Diana had finished her own check-in. I took one deep breath before going on.

"I just wanted to thank you for...well, thank you for saving my life," I told her. "I would not be in this world if it hadn't been for you. You held out hope for me when I had no hope. You believed in me when I was not able to believe in myself. And you...you loved me in a way I had never experienced love before. You taught me how to allow myself to be loved, and that love is really what saved my life."

I was smiling and crying at the same time, feeling a powerful sense of truth washing over me. I hadn't planned exactly what I was going to say to Diana, and the part about her love for me just spilled out unexpectedly. And it was true, my therapist loved me. I understood that as a general rule, mental health practitioners are trained to keep a professional distance when working with their patients and clients. Their emphasis is on diagnosing and treating problems, not bestowing pure love. And yet, while her therapeutic understanding and savvy interventions absolutely played their part, it was my therapist's love that ultimately made the difference in helping me say yes to life. In my work in learning to become the therapist I wanted to be, she had provided a profound lesson for me.

Diana just listened and watched me, and when I was done she crossed her hands and held them together, with her two thumbs pointed up. They looked like two little love wings. And then, without speaking a word, she simply nodded once and bowed.

For Diana, that bow was a simple, humble way of honoring my words. For me, it was a gesture that immediately poured in and found its permanent place in my soul.

14

The Cowgirl Rides Again

I've never completely lost contact with my mother, the person who brought me into this world in 1964 while still a very young and emotionally troubled woman herself. But I must admit that our contact has been, well, unusual I guess you could say. Over the course of many years, I would call her up once a month, and when she picked up the phone and heard my voice, she would immediately hang up. A month later I would do it again. Occasionally our little phone dance would take a break, and we would actually see each other once or twice within a couple of years' time before my mother retreated back to her hang-up routine.

So, what happened on that day several years ago when I had flown from Atlanta to visit her in Oregon could not have come as a bigger surprise to me.

"Come back here," she said. "I have something for you." She was ushering me toward the room that had once been my bedroom, before she and my stepfather shipped me out to Christie School to begin my long journey into dark and frightening places I still didn't like to think about. Although I could now step back into that old room without getting smacked with a wave of past trauma, I didn't exactly expect anything positive to emerge there either.

"Go on, take a look," she said, as I hesitated at the doorway.

Wow! In the middle of my former bedroom, mounted on a sawhorse, was a saddle wrapped with a bow. On the top of the saddle was a little shoe box with spurs popping out of it.

"It's yours," she said. "I want you to have it."

There was a story behind that saddle, and I knew it well. It had belonged to my great-grandmother Millie, the one who, according to our family stories, used to ride in the Pendleton Roundup, drawing ooh's and aah's from the large crowds with her cowgirl tricks as she stood up in the saddle. This saddle with my name on it had once belonged to her, and after a few family tugs-of-war, ownership had landed in my mother's lap. And now she was passing it along to me, the 40-something woman who as a young girl had tried to ride a horse a time or two in adventures that didn't exactly win applause and trophies.

Yep, I had once dreamed of being the cowgirl. And now, my mother was giving me another chance.

"This is amazing," I said as ran my fingers along the sides of my new gift. I didn't just mean the saddle itself. This was the most meaningful item my mother could ever give to me, a grand gesture that said, "You are a valuable human being, and I want to bestow this present on you as a way to acknowledge just how valuable you are to me. And I love you."

She offered to ship the saddle to me after I flew back to Atlanta, but I declined. Let's just say that her reputation for follow-though and reliability had not exactly cemented my trust in such matters. Her intentions were often good, but actions were another thing entirely.

"No, thanks," I said with a smile. "I'm taking this saddle with me."

I carried that big saddle and kerplunked it in the trunk of my rental car. After I left my mother that day, I drove right to the nearest shipping office and gladly paid the steep bill for sending it home.

Even before I landed in Atlanta, I knew exactly what I was going to do with my saddle. I was going to make it the centerpiece of my own personal cowgirl room in my home. Making curtains out of bark cloth and posting photos of the Pendleton Round-Up on the walls, I rode that horse and trick rider theme through the whole creation. It's a guest room now, but when no one is visiting us, I go in there often, just to admire my saddle and to reflect on my love of horses and my connection to family. I loved my adopted family dearly, but for better or worse I also recognized that I had a first family too. Even with all the trauma I had suffered living on the inside or the periphery of that family, it was important to keep it alive in my life. Doing so affirmed that I really did have roots, and although there were far too many experiences tied to those roots that I had to suffer through and eventually heal, there was still something worth celebrating.

For years when I was struggling with the identity of a mental health patient, I would wait and hope for my mother to apologize for the hurt and pain that had been dished out to me in my childhood. "Doesn't she see my wounds? Doesn't she understand how messed up this picture is? Doesn't she get it?" I would say over and over to myself. And then, long after I had given up the waiting and hoping, she sent me a letter. It wasn't a long letter, maybe five or six sentences, but it only took a few lines to transmit the message that was still important to me.

What I took from her letter was something that was still deeply important to me: acknowledgement. My mother had at last acknowledged some of her shortcomings and mistreatment. I found myself opening up to a much greater acceptance of who she was and her role in my life. She was only 18 when she got married and 19 when I came on the scene, a young mother in the wild and crazy 1960s who had to grapple with her own mental and emotional struggles. One way or another, she had done the best she could.

There were more surprises coming through the mother-daughter channel. After I made a subsequent, unannounced visit at my mother's home, she sent me a message in which she actually thanked me for stopping by. And on a recent birthday, she texted me, something I'm not sure she had ever done. She wished me a happy birthday and referred to me as "little girl." Amazing.

I even had a surprising moment with Jack during one of my visits to Oregon. Out of the blue, he pulled me aside and said, "I was a real jerk to you when you were young" although he used a more colorful word choice than "jerk."

"Well, that was a long time ago," I said. "I've moved on…but thank you for acknowledging that you were a jerk."

With a door apparently opening for further reconnection, I invited my mother and stepfather to come to Atlanta and see what my life looked like. Even though they seldom traveled, they said yes. One more surprise: I had a very enjoyable time showing them around.

I felt grateful that I had this opportunity to have meaningful contact with the two of them, so that they would not remain stuck in my mind as dark and demonic figures from my past. They are human beings, as we all are, and they made mistakes, as we all do. I try to remind myself of that, as I also try to stay aware of just how much I have to be grateful for in my life.

I have love in my life today, with a man with whom I share not only common goals and core beliefs but a deep spiritual connection. Some time ago, I happened to set up my dear friend Liz with the woman who has become her life partner. Another major joy is having Sarah very much in my life. I also get to share my love with three dogs, including my therapy dog Gracie Jane. When I have the time and energy, I am active in social justice issues, speaking out against poverty, racism, violence and other issues that affirm my values and provide another way to make a difference in the world.

I have been able to fulfill my goal to become a therapist, serving those whose lives have been weighed down by trauma. When I founded ThrivingHeart, I chose the name because it fits my own journey of growth and healing. My heart, for so long dark and wounded, was finally able to thrive.

The story of how I came upon the building where my staff and I serve our clients is another example of how much I have to be grateful for. When I moved to Atlanta because of a relationship I was in at the time, I first worked for the National Mental Health Association. I was involved with the development of a mental health outreach program, and I was visible and respected enough to be interviewed on CNN, and ABC's *World News Tonight*. That was certainly meaningful work, but my goal had always been to launch something of my own, once I had been in Atlanta long enough to understand the people and the Southern culture. For years I was co-leader of a training program called Heartwork, and then I reached the point of wanting to re-enter private practice and eventually create a vibrant healing arts entity.

During this time, I would drive by an old yellow Victorian house in Atlanta every day. Something about that building just magnetically pulled me in. "That's my place," I would say. "I'm supposed to be there." The only problem was, the house wasn't for sale. I just kept admiring it anyway, and held that image of owning that building and establishing my new center there. When the "For Sale" sign went up, I called immediately. That's when I learned that the asking price, which I figured would be a bit high because of neighborhood redevelopment, was several leagues above me. Maybe I would have to let go of that dream and find a new one.

One day around this time, I was having lunch with an entrepreneur who I knew professionally. Our meeting was part of my commitment to pick 12 people to meet with once a month each year, to build connections and glean ideas for how to launch and grow my own endeavors. I happened to tell this man about my obsession with that old house on the market.

"That's interesting," he said. "Did you find out who owns the property?"

"No," I replied, "I just called the broker on the for-sale sign."

"Sure, that makes sense," he went on. "Tell me more about what you want to do with the building."

I shared more about my vision to create my own place, to put together a team of healing-oriented practitioners, to serve not only children, adults and families in trauma, but under-served groups like the LGBT community. I wanted to be a beacon of hope for the abandoned, the wounded and the neglected—and anyone with a deep need for compassionate therapeutic guidance.

"Do you really want to know who owns that building?" he asked.

"Yeah, I guess. Sure," I said.

"I do."

"What? Really?"

"Really. So, you very much want that building, right? And you would make a deal today if you could?"

"Well, sure, but like I told you, I can't afford it. Not even close. I couldn't even come up with the deposit."

"Never mind all that. Listen, I've always seen that space as a potential little diamond in the community. Everything you're telling me about what you want to do there fits perfectly with what I had in mind. Kristine, if you really want to buy that building, we'll make it happen."

By then I was in tears. We firmed up the details before lunch was over, and after a new paint job for the outside and a redesign to meet our needs inside, I launched my dream center: ThrivingHeart Healing Arts Associates. I had one more treasured component of my life to hold in gratitude.

There are so many other examples, including how I changed my name. That transformation dates back to my days as a student in Seattle in the '90s. I did not want my diploma to have either the last name of my birth family or my stepfather on it. Also, I yearned for a first name that sounded more adult, more powerful than Kristy or Kris. Kristine felt like a natural shift there, but coming up with the right last name called for a bit of research. With a friend's help, I perused a book of women's mythology. After trimming the prospects to eight nominees, I turned to the same process that landed me in Seattle: writing the names on eight different index cards and putting them under my pillow overnight. In the morning, "Medea" leaped out as the winner. To clarify, my association with the name aligned with the original reputation of the Goddess Medea as a figure of wisdom with a proficiency for healing others, not the much later myth in which Medea kills her children. I added the middle name Grace to anchor that quality in my life, reminding me to always seek to move about the world with grace.

I began using my new name even before leaving Seattle, but it was never legal or official. I decided to take that step in Atlanta several years later. That threw me into a complex legal process, and I was getting frustrated at times with all the hoops to jump through. The trail included having my new name posted in a court newspaper for six weeks, before I finally got a court date, three days before Christmas. When the appointed day arrived, the judge asked me to see him in his chambers.

"So, tell me exactly why you want this change," he said firmly, and for just a second I flashed to other judges and other courts where I was treated harshly and nothing seemed within my control.

"Well, um, that is…you see," I began, stumbling with my words and looking at this judge for any sign of compassion. He just looked… neutral. Then I decided to just go on and tell him. "I grew up in the foster care system and when I was Kristy I was a runaway, a mental patient and many other things I would forget if I could," I went on, and I added enough detail to bolster my case without sounding like I was seeking pity. When I stopped talking, he looked at me intently for a few seconds before speaking.

"Name change granted," he said, and then he smiled. "And Merry Christmas."

At the risk of sounding corny, I have to say that sometimes I almost feel like pinching myself and asking, "Is this really *my* life?" Sometimes when Liz and I are together, we laugh and imagine that if somebody had taken my file from childhood through my mid-20s and asked anyone to predict the future of "that girl," they would never have predicted anything close to my reality. No, this wasn't supposed to be my story. That girl who had been trampled in abuse, neglected, labeled and given up on was clearly writing a very different kind of story. But even in the worst of times, I believe I was on some kind of quest, a quest for my life. And, blessed by so much love and support from so many people, I fulfilled that quest.

With so much to be grateful for in my life, I'm always seeking opportunities to express my gratitude. One night, not so many years ago, I woke up at 3 a.m., with a clear and compelling urge: I had to contact WWIN. I had never properly thanked them for their generous and vital contribution to my education, and my future. I was hoping that it wasn't too late.

In the light of dawn, with tears pouring down, I drafted an email to Deborah, the executive director. I didn't worry about using the right words, just spoke from my heart about how thankful I was for what they had done. Their grant, coming at such a welcome time, had enabled me to take a breath and finish my education with far less stress. I described my current-day professional work and apologized for not sending this note of gratitude earlier.

Deborah responded right away, thanking me for reaching out and asking me for permission to share my email with the organization's Board of Directors. Of course I said yes, and the next thing I knew, I was being invited to deliver the keynote address at their next major fundraising event in Seattle. What an opportunity!

As I prepared my talk, "Bearing Witness: My Life So Far in 10 Short Chapters," I discovered that this speech was giving me a chance to express my gratitude not only to WWIN but to other key supporters on my journey. I told the audience about Mrs. Holycross, my kind and caring fourth grade teacher who came to my home to continue to teach me after I had been expelled from school for violent and disruptive behavior. I told them about Gary, who took me to dinner to celebrate my birthday and assured me that I had a future and it wasn't as a mental patient.

Doing my best to keep my emotions at bay, I went on to tell them about Bev and how she first rescued me from the back of that Chevy Nova in an ice storm and how she had loved me and stood up for me, time and time again. Then I told them about Diana, and how she had challenged the labels that defined me and stood in the fire with me in the face of deep sorrow and a near-lethal suicide attempt, always believing that I could indeed find my way and eventually thrive. I also told them about my deep friendship with Liz, who kept supporting and encouraging me, insisting that I really deserved an education and that I was smart enough to achieve it.

After acknowledging the trust, confidence and hands-on guidance provided to me by the Leadership Institute of Seattle, I turned my attention toward thanking WWIN.

"Never had I encountered such a humble and generous organization," I said. "You treated me like a human being, extending sincere encouragement and respect along with the grant, and I walked away from this experience believing more in myself and my future.

"Let me tell you what can happen when a community comes together with a belief that investing in a woman like me is worthwhile. Belief can strengthen our community. It is like a ripple in the pond of life… You never know how far that one act of generosity will reach or how many lives that one action will touch."

Apparently, my talk had a very positive impact on the fundraising mission. When Deborah called to thank me for speaking, she shared her excitement at the overwhelming response from the attendees at the fundraiser. "Can you come speak at our next one?" she asked. Which, of course, I did. The way I look at it, we can never have too many opportunities to say thank you. Especially when it may be our last chance to do so…

Bev had been seriously ill for a while when my sisters and I planned a girls' trip for her. We were going to put her in a bed in a big RV and head to Kahn-Nee-Ta, a resort and spa on the edge of a Native American reservation in eastern Oregon. A couple of days before that adventure was due to launch, I got the phone call late in the evening. It was time to come.

After frantically searching for an airline reservation out of Atlanta that night and coming up empty, I reached out to the friend who was always there for me. "Don't worry about it. I will call you back when I've got it worked out," Liz said when I filled her in on the crisis. The only way it worked was to follow a crazy itinerary from Atlanta to San Francisco to Portland. All along the route, I would call periodically. "Is she still with us?" I asked. Please don't die before I get there.

When I got to her room, Bev opened her eyes. I told the rest of the family, many of whom had been keeping a vigil for hours and hours without sleep, that they could take a break. Leaning in close, I patted Bev on the head and took a breath.

"You know, I haven't had you long enough," I said, "but I understand that it's your time. I'll be okay, everybody will be okay. But right now, I just have to tell you something. I would not be who I am today if it had not been for you and everything that you have done for me. So thank you. Thank you for loving me."

15

No Bad Apples

I carry two vivid images from my return visit to Oregon State Hospital that I mentioned in the Introduction to this book.

The first image emerged from seeing the toybox of Ward 40A, an aquarium-sized plexiglass container kept under lock and key until those rare occasions when the children patients were allowed access to it and could play with whatever they could find in there. That toybox was still there when I entered the now-closed children's and adolescent unit as an adult, and when I looked inside I noticed only a couple of teddy bears left behind. Fighting back tears, I took a quick picture.

Those teddy bears triggered a rush of sadness, not only for myself but for all the children who had once lived there. It was such a sad place, full of lonely and hurt kids. None of us felt like we belonged in a state hospital, or that we belonged anywhere really. We were outcast children, like teddy bears unclaimed by potentially loving owners, left behind forever.

The second image came to me while I was standing next to a cabinet in the Rec area. The hospital staff used to keep board games in that cabinet, but only a single game remained now. I read the name, "One Bad Apple," along with "40A" written on the cover to identify our ward.

I don't recall playing that game, except perhaps once or twice, but I do remember that name. One Bad Apple.

That was me, or at least how I seemed to be regarded by most of the staff at Oregon State Hospital and all the other psychiatric facilities, courts, juvenile jails, schools, foster homes and emergency shelters where I had left my mark. I was the bad girl, the one who always seemed to be getting into trouble. When I wasn't shoving some student or teacher in school, I was swearing at judges in court. Or running away from wherever I was being kept while hell-bent on living on my own terms, even if that meant prostituting myself on the streets of the city. Or flying into a screaming fit that would wind up with grim-faced staff holding me down and forcing me into restraints.

As the bad apple, I was looked upon as the problem, the "it" that had to be fixed. I was emotionally disturbed, unsocialized, crazy. Every snapshot of my behavior was to be captured and analyzed as evidence of my current state and the plans the professionals would make for my future.

Those were the memories that came flooding back about 10 years ago when I was finally back inside the place that served as my home as a 13-year-old girl, a child rejected by her family and unable to fit in any kind of box the caregivers would try to keep her in. It was a cold and often brutal home. Not long ago, I came across a reference that lobotomies were still being performed on patients at the Oregon State Hospital as late as 1983, several years after my time living there.

I don't blame the individuals involved in my treatment. During my earlier re-visit to Oregon State Hospital, under the cover of a professional researcher studying the adult-life effects of institutionalized care on children, I had an opportunity to sit face-to-face with a few of the staff from Ward 40A who had a hand in the care of the young patients during my time there. I found them pleasant, kind, well-spoken, and seemingly guided by the best of intentions. They had devoted long professional careers to the cause of helping children.

That was a welcome realization for me, because I never wanted to demonize everyone charged with my supervision and care. They were simply executing roles in a system that, rather than truly help me to heal, to grow, to believe in myself and to chart a new and positive direction in life, just contributed to my pain. They took the trauma that I had already suffered growing up in an unhealthy family and added layers and layers of new trauma, the trauma that comes from being forced to reside in the darkest corridors of the mental health system.

But as painful as those images and memories still can be for me, I don't look back at everything that happened before, during, and after my life as a patient in the state hospital with resentment. Not at all. Strange as it may sound, I'm actually thankful for everything that happened to me back then, appreciative of living in the dark and frightening world that I was forced to face and somehow endure. Why? Because all along the way, I was in training to become a therapist, a professional uniquely equipped with the experience, understanding, and awareness of what it means to pay the price of childhood trauma.

I regard myself as a Wounded Healer. I'm the girl who was put through the fire and came out a strong, determined woman committed to assisting others as they forge their way through their own pain and turmoil. I would not be able to do the work that I do, in the way that I do it, if I didn't have my personal history. As I sometimes joke with my colleagues, "I'm glad I had all my training before I went to school." It's true that there was a great deal of harm that I suffered, but it's equally true that I learned how to move from the place of being a victim of that suffering to the place of surviving and ultimately thriving. So, when I sit with clients who have been knocked down by trauma today, I not only can resonate with where they are but also glimpse the possible future they may attain. I hold out a vision of hope and possibility. I can tell them this:

You are not alone. Know that no matter what has happened to you, your life is worth living. We can embark on a new journey together. We're going to work to clear your path of the trauma that has been blocking it and pave the way toward a rich life, a life worth living, however you may define it. Allow yourself to start imagining what you want, how you want to feel, how you want to be in relationship with yourself, with those around you, with the world. We'll find your new path. I don't know exactly what it will look like or where it will take you, but we will get you there.

Much of what happens in my work revolves around the healing of a wounded heart. More often than not, that heart was first wounded when they were abandoned, neglected, rejected or mistreated by family or caregivers in their childhood home. As someone who was thrown out of her own childhood nest, I can assure them that they have the potential to learn to fly, if they find the tribe that will help them navigate their way.

All healing happens through relationship, at least to a certain degree. Those who have been wounded desperately need the experience of being close to someone who deeply cares about them, loves them and will dedicate themselves to their well-being. Sometimes when I am privileged to witness the healing and growth, and the exciting new directions followed by those who have successfully traveled through trauma, I remember back to when the switch flipped for me and I began to fully claim a healthy and fulfilling life after my attempted suicide. Maybe, in a spiritual light, I finally said yes to life because I was being called to do this healing work with others. It is my vocation and my passion.

I'm just as passionate when I speak out for changes in our mental health system in the way that we look at and treat young people. Some things have changed since the days that I was made a ward of the state of Oregon and pushed down the rabbit hole of traumatic mental health treatment, but much remains unchanged. Children struggling with emotional and psychological issues are still pathologized, still identified as "sick" or "bad" and needing to be "fixed." Not nearly enough attention is paid to the need to integrate active therapeutic work with the family of those children from unhealthy home environments. All too often these kids who have been wounded at home are abandoned or shamed, rather than being understood and embraced as human beings with the potential to change and grow—if their professional caregivers commit themselves to get the growing part going.

Children in psychiatric facilities are still medicated, though the popular drugs have different names and doses. When their behavior does not fit the rules and structure of their treatment facility, they are still restrained, even if the apparatus used to perform that function goes by a more kid-friendly term like "burrito sack." Even when the intentions of caregivers are positive, the structure of the environment in which treatment is delivered typically creates an Us-versus-Them dynamic. And within that dynamic, there is little or no room for love.

It saddens and frustrates me that most professionals in our field are taught that they must never become emotionally involved with the young people they are entrusted to help. They learn to maintain a professional attitude and posture, to believe that they always know what is best for these girls and boys. Their role is simply to treat them, to try to make them less sick. As someone who would not be here today were it not for the love bestowed on me by caregivers like Gary and Diana who had the courage to open their hearts and weave love into the tapestry of their professional work, I reject that belief. Children and young adults who wind up in the treatment offices and hospital rooms of psychological and psychiatric caregivers need caring and, yes, love from these therapists, psychiatrists and counselors as much or more as they need their professional expertise and therapeutic guidance. They cry out for meaningful human connection, often the foundation for any successful intervention.

I'm encouraged when I am reminded that I am not alone in recognizing and addressing the need for a more compassionate and human approach to the mental health treatment of children. Several years ago, I was deeply honored to be invited to speak at a symposium on mental health policy and treatment hosted by former First Lady Rosalynn Carter at the Carter Center in Atlanta. I utilized this wonderful opportunity to shine a critical spotlight on the limitations and inherent harm in pathologizing children and the value of seeking more holistic approaches:

> **It is essential to bridge the personal and professional in order to develop authentic relationships with children in care. As professionals, we cannot walk the journey of recovery for children and their families. Yet we can hold the light to guide**

them on their path, being mindful to reflect back to them that they are lovable and that there is a place for them in the world where their full expression of self is welcome and honored. We can hold the vision of hope when they cannot.

Then I shared the story of a girl named Kristy, punctuating the details of my despair in institutional care with the lighter note that began, "Had you told Kristy at age 10 or 12 or even 25 that she would one day share a stage with Rosalynn Carter and other esteemed advocates for the rights and well-being of children, she would have thought that perhaps you should be locked up right there beside her." I also acknowledged that others dedicated to the mental health care of children also have suffered:

> Many of us have stories to tell. Many of us, or those that we love, were children who were forgotten, discarded, and in some instances destroyed by the systems charged with our care. How do we bring the fullness of our personal history and experience to our professional work in a way that is both respectful and respected? How do we model well for the children who we work with the potential for survival, recovery, and redemption, for a life worth living? How do we build on the good and innovative work that has begun and inculcate change in all the systems that are raising children in this country?

> My message is simple really. We must incorporate into our treatment of families and children an acknowledgment of the importance of personal and community connection, the value of story and of being witnessed, the need for understanding of family history and legacy, and the firm belief that the possibility of growth, healing and an enriching life exists in everyone.

In other words, there are no bad apples. There are only children and young adults who, no matter how bad or sick or crazy they may appear to others, are inherently worthy of our understanding, patience, compassionate care and love. Bell Hooks, in her book *Salvation: Black*

People and Love, reminds us that "Only love can give us the strength to go forward in the midst of heartbreak and misery. Only love can give us the power to reconcile, to redeem, the power to renew weary spirits and save lost souls. The transformative power of love is the foundation of all meaningful social change. Without love our lives are without meaning. Love is the heart of the matter. When all else falls away, love sustains."

If you ever find yourself with an opportunity to offer caring and support to a young person in the midst of trauma and despair, my hope is that you will always remember that healing power of love. And if you are a child, adolescent or young adult caught in the throes of deep pain and suffering, my wish for you is that you will be welcomed by those who can provide that kind of healing love, and that one day you will be able to unveil and embrace your thriving heart.

Afterword

As I was editing this book, I found myself in Portland, surrounded by my birth family as I shepherded my 99-year-old grandpa on to his next adventure. He was my favorite family member, the one who for so long was my touchstone, and a reminder that there was more of where I came from than what I experienced and lost.

Immersed in this book and my birth family—Mom, Jack, Karen—flush with so many stories and memories, I was struck by the absurdity of so many parts of this story and the stories not yet told...and of so many parts of my life. If I hadn't lived through it myself, I'm not sure I'd believe it all.

And I realized that the word absurd didn't even appear in these pages. Until now.

ab·surd
/əbˈsərd,əbˈzərd/

adjective
wildly unreasonable, illogical, or inappropriate
"my life was completely absurd"
synonyms: preposterous, ridiculous, ludicrous...

Made in the USA
Columbia, SC
29 May 2018